LPL: A Structured Language for Modeling Linear Programs

Europäische Hochschulschriften
Publications Universitaires Européennes
European University Studies

Reihe V
Volks- und Betriebswirtschaft

Série V   Series V
Sciences économiques, gestion d'entreprise
Economics and Management

Band/Vol. 865

PETER LANG
Bern · Frankfurt am Main · New York · Paris

Tony Hürlimann

LPL:
A STRUCTURED LANGUAGE
FOR MODELING
LINEAR PROGRAMS

PETER LANG
Bern · Frankfurt am Main · New York · Paris

CIP-Kurztitelaufnahme der Deutschen Bibliothek

Hürlimann, Tony:
LPL: a structured language for modeling linear
programs / Tony Hürlimann.– Bern; Frankfurt am Main;
New York; Paris: Lang, 1987.
(European university studies; Ser. 5,
Economics and management; Vol. 865)
ISBN 3-261-03793-8

NE: Europäische Hochschulschriften / 05

© Verlag Peter Lang AG, Bern 1987
Nachfolger des Verlages der
Herbert Lang & Cie AG, Bern

Druck: Weihert-Druck GmbH, Darmstadt

Contents

I

Mit der Annahme einer Dissertation beabsichtigt die rechts-, wirtschafts- und
sozialwissenschaftliche Fakultät der Universität Freiburg nicht, zu den darin enthaltenen
wissenschaftlichen Meinungen des Verfassers Stellung zu nehmen.
(Fakultätsbeschluss vom 1. Juli 1916)

Some bookes are to bee tasted,

others to bee swallowed,

and some few to bee chewed and disgested.

-- FRANCIS BACON, *Essayes (1597)*

Preface

During the last four decades, Operations Research has concentrated considerable effort on designing techniques for solving linear programming (LP) models. Research in this field, coupled with progress in computer technology, now allow us to solve large and complex LP models. Another topic in modeling, surprisingly neglected, is model management. Only recently have we witnessed an increasing development of tools for model building, analysis and documentation. The goal of this dissertation is to contribute to this development.

More specifically, the main objective of this dissertation is to present a new modeling language, called **LPL**. LPL may be used to build, modify and document large, live LP models. The development of the LPL language was motivated by practical modeling tasks. For nearly 10 years, a research group at the University of Fribourg has been charged, by the Swiss government, with the task of planning a comprehensive analysis of the alimentary self-sufficiency of Switzerland in the case of a severe international crisis. Since World War II, this self-sufficiency is considered as one of the fundamental elements of Swiss security policy and the results of this planning have important consequences on Swiss agricultural policy.

In the above context and in order to offer an in-depth illustration of an LPL program, various parts of the large LP model, namely the EP model, which served as the major impetus behind the development of the LPL language, are formulated and exposed in Appendix 3.

Any attempt to thoroughly acknowledge the contributions and guidance I received from colleagues would be inadequate. A few people stand out, however, and deserve a special thanks. Professor Dr. J. Kohlas, who initially suggested that I develop a modeling language and who offered me many valuable hints along the way; Dr. P. Hättenschwiler, who's experience in practical model building was particularly helpful, he gave me the idea to link the modeling language with a database system; and Dr. G. Egli, who developed the fundamental ideas of the LPN representation.. I would like to thank Professor Dr. J.-P. Boss who kindly accepted to be the second reader of this dissertation. I would also like to express my sincere appreciation to Jane Pasquier for direct help in carefully reading the manuscript.

There persists an overwhelming frustration in modeling large LP problems. The analyst must work for months to build, document, verify and input the model into a computer, in order to finally have a solution after just a few minutes of running time on a mainframe computer. When considering how to employ a computer for modeling, there is a tendency to limit the scope to database management and the appropriate solution procedures. Model building, model verification and modification are still painful, primarily manual work with high overall costs. This may be a reason, that Operations Research techniques still find a limited usage in commercial practice.

For small models, such as those which may be interesting for teaching LP techniques, there exist many excellent LP software packages on personal computers. Large LP's, however, with hundreds or thousands of variables which represent real environments and which are thus, relevant in practice, present us with a new range of problems. The very convenient matrix representation, for instance, is no longer applicable due to severe problems of *storage*. To store the entire matrix of 2'000 rows and 5'000 columns with an accuracy of 8 bytes per entry, would require more then 80 Mb (megabytes) of space. Fortunately most large scale LP's have sparse matrix density and other representations of the model, like the standard MPSX form would, therefore, take much less space on the disk. Another problem lies in the area of *error searching*, (i.e., for infeasibility). The *overview* of a large LP is rapidly rendered unsuitable, if no special tools are built around the LP. Finally, the sticky problem concerning *nomenclature* is sometimes overlooked. Each row and column should have a unique name and since these names cannot exceed eight characters in most software packages, they must be carefully planned. Subtle abbreviations must be invented. These are only few examples of problems stemming from the manipulation of large LP models.

The continuing need for the construction, modification, adaptation and documentation of medium to large size LP models has led to the development and use of a number of modeling tools. Examples of such tools for model management are:

Matrix Generators: Matrix Generators have been the predominant tools used to produce a standard input file of large linear programs for the computer. Some are widely used, whereas others have been built for special models only. One of these Matrix Generator techniques is particularly interesting because it is based on the database programming language, dBASEII. This technique allows the modeler to create the entire MPSX file for a specific model with some dBASEII tables (Pasquier J., 1986). We will take a look at some of the other prominent Matrix Generators in Chapter 2. *Report Generators* treat the output and are useful for tabulating the results.

Graphs: Some LP's are best represented by graphs. Riggs introduces the RPM (Resource Planning and Management) network consisting of resource and process nodes, source and sink nodes and the relationships between these nodes (Riggs, 1975 pp. 65). Another powerful tool for graphic documentation for large LP's is called **LPN** (Linear Programming Network) and has been developed and used by Egli (Egli 1980). The LPN is further discussed in Chapter 4. Similar graphs for analysis have also been considered by Greenberg (Greenberg 1982).

Modeling Languages: An alternative tool is presented in this dissertation. An efficient and readable modeling language called LPL (Linear Programming Language) allows an LP problem to be formulated in terms familiar to an analyst. The fundamental idea behind LPL is to be able to write an LP in a concise, symbolic form, close to the algebraic notation for variables, constraints and objectives, and to leave as much of the work as possible to the machine. The machine in this sense, translates the symbolic form into a coded form like the standard MPSX file. An LPL compiler, which performs this translation, is available. Several tools, exposed in Chapter 5, have also been built around this compiler in order to consider the model from different vantage points. The development of LP modeling languages is a recent phenomenon. R. Fourer mentions in his paper (Fourer 1983), the interesting, hypothetical XML modeling language, which is similar to our own attempts. In contrast to LPL, however, the indexing mechanism in XML is more restrictive and does not provide for the possibility of reading data directly from databases. Other modeling languages have been developed and are presented in Chapter 2.

2

Matrix Generators & Modeling Languages

2.1 DEFINITION OF AN LP MODEL

Using matrix notation, the linear programming (LP) problem may be stated in the following form:

$$\text{Maximize} \quad M = c'x \quad (\sum_{j=1}^{n} c_j x_j \quad \text{where } j = \{1...n\} \ ) \quad (2\text{-}1)$$

$$\text{subject to} \quad r: Ax = b \quad (\sum_{j=1}^{n} a_{ij} x_j = b_i \quad \text{where } i = \{1...m\} \ ) \quad (2\text{-}2)$$

$$x >= 0 \quad (\quad x_j >= 0 \ ) \quad (2\text{-}3)$$

M in Eq. (2-1) is called the *objective function* r in Eq. (2-2) is called the *constraint* or *restriction*; c' is the transposed *cost vector*; A is an mxn data matrix; b is the *right-hand side vector* and x represents the *variable vector*.

The matrix form defined above is called the *primal problem*. For each LP there exists a corresponding *dual problem*. The optimal values of these two problems are the same. The two problems are at their most symmetrical when presented in the so-called *canonical form*, as shown below:

$$\text{Minimize} \quad M' = b'r \quad (\sum_{i=1}^{m} b_i r_i \ ) \quad (2\text{-}4)$$

$$\text{subject to} \quad x: A'r = c \quad (\sum_{i=1}^{m} a_{ij} r_i = c_j \ ) \quad (2\text{-}5)$$

$$r >= 0 \quad (2\text{-}6)$$

3

2.2 PRESENTATION OF AN LP MODEL

The matrix notation is a concise, convenient form used to point out theoretical aspects

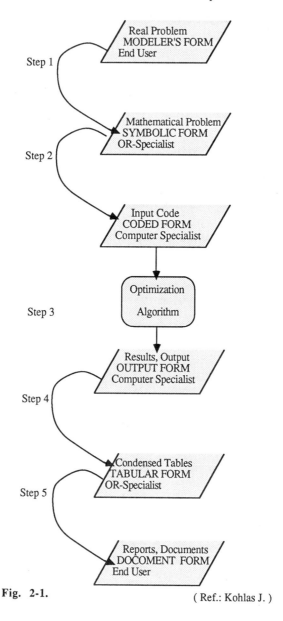

Fig. 2-1.   (Ref.: Kohlas J.)

of any LP problem. Abstractly speaking, the goal of the formulation process of a specific LP model is to provide numerical values for **A**, **b** and **c** and to develop labeling schemes for the row- and column-names. In large-scale models, however, this formulation process is a difficult and expensive task. Fig. 2-1 demonstrates the different steps through which the modeling process must pass.

Step 1 is essentially a conceptual task. A concrete model formulation must be transformed into a symbolic form, which may be a network representation or an explicit mathematical form.

Step 2 is purely mechanical, but generally time-consuming. Unique row- and column names must be invented, the data must be copied from tables and the code must be entered in a computer in a prescribed form. Traditional approaches divide the work in Step 2 between modeler and machine. First, the symbolic form is converted to a special computer program, then this program is executed by the computer in order to produce the desired coded form. This intermediate computer program is known as a *Matrix Generator*. A quite different approach to this translation is the *modeling language*. A modeling language is a declarative language that expresses the model in a symbolic form which the computer can interpret directly.

Step 3 is then performed automatically by the computer and results in a standard output code. This output is, generally, a long list of results, which must be condensed into tabular form to be readable.

Step 4 is this condensing task and is performed by a *Report Generator*.

In Step 5, documents and reports must then be produced in order to make the model comprehensible to managers or other end users involved in analyzing the results.

2.3 AN HISTORICAL OVERVIEW

A variety of tools to facilitate LP formulations have been proposed in recent years.

2.3.1 Matrix Generators

Some existing matrix generators are listed below. No attempt is made to treat them individually. Detailed information may be found in the corresponding references: IBM MGRW (IBM 1972), APEX-II MRG (Control Data 1974), DATAFORM (Ketron 1975), DATAMAT (M.I.T. 1975), MAGEN (Haverly 1976), GAMMA (Sperry 1977), OMNI (Haverly 1977), MODELER (Burroughs 1980). These matrix generators are also mentioned in Fourer's paper (Fourer 1983).

The philosophies of design are quite similar. The major structural points which each of these matrix generators have in common are:

5

- lists and tables of data and row- and column-names must be prepared in a special format,
- a program, written in a matrix generator language often similar to FORTRAN must then be created and serves to process the lists and tables,
- some loop statements or matrix operations are generally included in the language in order to process a whole table with one statement,
- detailed instructions must be given to produce the row-, column- and right-hand side section of the MPSX format. Therefore, the programmer requires a detailed knowledge of the computer produced, coded form.

Matrix generators are certainly a great advance over translation by human labor alone. Nevertheless, there are substantial drawbacks inherent in their use. Transparency is lost and data handling is inflexible. Writing a matrix generator program is more a job for programmers then for modelers. New errors may be included while writing the program. To verify, if a computer produced, coded form is a correct translation of its symbolic form is not an easy job. Further documentation must be produced to describe the matrix generator. All this extra work is not a fundamental part of LP modeling.

2.3.2 Network Representations

Some LP's are best described by graphs. A very well-known representation of special LP's - the generalized transshipment problem - is the *generalized network* (GN) introduced by Glover (Glover 1973). A generalized transshipment problem is an LP, which has in each column of its matrix **A**, no more than two coefficients different from zero (all others are zero). The precise definition of a generalized transshipment problem is found in (Brandenberger 1984 p.11). A GN is represented as a (directed) graph with m nodes (the constraints) and n arcs (the variables). Two nodes are connected by an arc, if and only if in the corresponding column of the matrix **A** the coefficients are non-zeros. (see Brandenberger 1984 and Glover 1981). General LP models, however, cannot be represented by GN's.

Riggs exposes the RPM-network (Resource Planning and Management Network), which contains four components: resource nodes, symbolized by circles; process nodes, representing activities transforming resources from one form to another and symbolized by squares; minimizing source and maximizing sink nodes, representing the system's environment and symbolized by triangles pointing right; and structures representing relationships between the nodes, and symbolized by arrows indicating the technological constraints (Riggs 1975 p. 66). Although any LP may be formulated by a RPM-network, this representation is limited to small LP's, due to its one to one representation and its rigid, semantical interpretation of the basic elements.

The Linear Programming Network (LPN), proposed by Egli (Egli 1980), is another

6

powerful graphical tool used to represent the structure of an LP. Due to its index mechanism, it is possible to represent large LP's. The LPN has already been used in practical model building for documentation. It will be further discussed in Chapter 4.

The reason that graphical representations are mentioned here, is that in the future, interactive, *graphics editors* may be built to model LP problems. A graphics editor is a type of software which permits the modeler to draw the graphical representation of a model on a screen just as he would have previously designed his model on paper. The graph on the screen is then directly interpreted by the computer. As personal computers and work-stations become more powerful, graphics editors may be more readily implemented. To the best of my knowledge such a tool does not presently exist. The LPN offers some basic principles for constructing a graphics editor.

2.3.3 Modeling Languages

Many modeling languages have now been implemented. For a detailed survey see Fourer (Fourer 1983). They may be divided into two main groups: 1) languages, which do not incorporate any kind of symbolic indexing and which are, thus, intended mainly for teaching and small-scale modeling, and 2) more sophisticated languages, which offer the symbolic indexing feature.

The first group includes: SSUPAC (Aigner 1967), UHELP (Donaghey 1970), EZLP (Jarvis 1976), EASYLP (see Rothenberg 1979 pp. 267), LINDO (Schrage 1981), LP83 (Sunset 1985). This list is not exhaustive. Most of these languages have integrated solution procedures and links to spreadsheets (LP83 to LOTUS 123). Generally, in an interactive session, the model is entered into a computer constraint by constraint, similar to an arithmetic notation. Sharda gives an excellent survey of commercially available LP packages for micro-computers (Sharda 1984).

The following languages fall into the second category mentioned above: ALPS (Steinberg 1977), LMC (Mills 1977), a general matrix generator (Anthonisse 1979), LPMODEL (Katz 1980), GAMS (Bischop 1981), UIMP (Ellison 1982), MGG/VM (SCICON 1984), MAGIC/LAMPS (Forrest 1984) and PAM . Once again, this list is not exhaustive.

LPMODEL is an interactive system written in APL. The philosophy of this language is quite close to that of LPL: the indices are first entered in a natural way (non-numerical subscripts), then data are assigned to subscripted identifiers and constraints are written in algebraic notation. Unfortunately, LPMODEL seems to be limited to small LP's. Appendix 3 gives the example used by Katz in an LPL notation (see CROP.LPL). UIMP is a more complex and powerful language. Three or even four dimensional data-tables may be defined in a compact, readable form. The production of internal row- and column-names is well-designed and the formulation of constraints is close to algebraic notation. The language syntax, however, is cumbersome and the associated programs are not easy to read. A great deal of programming code must be written to formulate an LP. The example used by Ellison takes more then two pages. The same model is formulated with LPL in this dissertation (see the model PRODUCT.LPL or PRODUCT1.LPL). MGG is another powerful tool similar to UIMP. The example used in the above reference is also written in LPL in Appendix 2 (see TRAVEL.LPL). MAGIC is closer to true matrix notation. Subunits of the matrix are built with the powerful OVER operator. The matrix may be build row- or columnwise. The formulation of the transportation problem mentioned by Forrest was also written in LPL (see SHIP.LPL or SHIP1.LPL). One of the recent and most powerful implementation is the fully table-oriented PAM. Appendix shows an example (see TRANS.LPL) which compares PAM with LPL.

Most of the languages noted above are offered as entire LP software packages with solution procedures and report writers.

Recent developments have attempted to include decision support systems (DSS) or artificial intelligence (AI) techniques to formulate large LP models. These first attempts have been outlined by Murphy (Murphy 1986).

Chapter 3

The LPL Modeling Language

3.1 INTRODUCTION

The philosophy behind LPL is quite simple. The model is formulated in a syntax close to algebraic notation with a powerful index mechanism. No knowledge of the coded form is necessary. The main features included in LPL and in contrast to other modeling languages are:

- a simple syntax close to the actual way that the modeler thinks about his model, and directly applicable for documentation (this is true also for LPMODEL),
- formulation of both small *and* large LP's (true also for UIMP, MGG and MAGIC),
- availability of a powerful, hierarchical index mechanism, making the model structuring very flexible,
- direct reading of data from dBASEII or dBASEIII files,
- automatic creation of the required dBASE database file structures, if the data are not yet available,
- automatic, user-controlled production of row- and column-names (problem of nomenclature) (true also for UIMP, MGG),
- tools for debugging the model (explicit equation listing, picture of the matrix and others),
- built-in text editor to enter the LPL program,
- fast production of the MPSX file.

The presently implemented LPL compiler does not contain:
- LPN graphics editor and LPN plot functions,
- problem analysis with the aid of the graph theory as discussed in chapter 4.7. (LPN and CAA),
- solution procedures for optimization.

3.2 BASIC OBJECTS

3.2.1 Basic Objects of an LP Model

Each LP model consists of the following elements: variables, constraints, coefficients, right-hand sides and an objective function. In the matrix notation (2-1 to 2-3), variables are represented by x. Coefficients and right-hand sides are numerical values called the *data* of the model. They are the two vectors b and c and the matrix A. The constraints and the objective function are linear (in)equations written in algebraic notation. Any LP can be expressed by these elements. Strictly speaking, all of these elements are composed elements: the variables x, for example, contains n individual variables: x_1, x_2, ... ,x_{n-1}, x_n. The individual element of each of these composed elements is called a *basic object*.

3.2.2 The LPL Alphabet

Basic objects in LPL have a certain syntax. Before exposing this syntax, the LPL alphabet must be introduced. It consists of the following characters:

Letters:	A to Z, a to z and _ (underscore)
Digits:	0 1 2 3 4 5 6 7 8 9
Special symbols:	+ - * / = < > ( ) [ ] { } . , : ; ' # &

No distinction is made between upper and lower case letters.

Reserved words are an integral part of LPL. They must, therefore, never be used as user-defined identifiers. The reserved words are:

coef end filetable forall like maketable
max min model program res set sum var

LPL programs are written entirely in printable ASCII characters as the alphabet shows. This allows them to be handled as ordinary text files.

3.2.3 Basic Language Objects of LPL

The basic objects of an LP are expressed in LPL by identifiers and real numbers. Variables, constraints and the objective function names are represented in LPL by *identifiers*. They have the same syntax as identifiers in other high level programming languages like PASCAL: a beginning letter or an underscore followed by letters, digits or underscores. An identifier may have any length, but only the first 15 characters are recognized. Like in PASCAL lower- and uppercase letters are not distinguished. 'Quantity', 'xv2' and 'FR_T_4' are three legal identifiers.

The data are represented by *real numbers* or arithmetic expressions of real numbers. Their range is between 1E-38 and 1E+38 with a mantissa of up to 11 significant digits.

10

'56', '-87.87687', '876765.7654' are examples of legal real numbers in LPL.
Operators can be used in order to write the linear constraints in an algebraic notation. They fall into four categories, which are listed below in order of precedence:

Unary Minus (for negative numbers only)
Multiplying Operators: * (times) and / (divide)
Adding Operators: + (plus) and - (minus)
Relational Operators: = , < , > , <= and >=

An LPL program has a free format and always includes two sections: a Declaration Section and a Model Section. In the Declaration Section all objects like coefficients (the data) and variables are declared, whereas in the Model Section all constraints (including the maximizing or minimizing function) are listed in algebraic form.

The following LPL program is an explicit representation of a very simple linear program with three variables named 'x', 'y' and 'z', two constraints named 'Restriction1' and 'Restriction2' and a maximizing objective function named 'Objective'. The program contains several comments, which can be included anywhere in the program. Like in PASCAL commands must be embedded within (* .. *) or within { .. }.

```
(* MODEL1.LPL: a simple LP-Model with three variables
   x,y and z, two restrictions and a minimizing
   objective function written in LPL. *)
(****************************************************)

{Variable Declaration}
var
  x y z

{Model Section}
model
  Restriction1: x + 43*y = 4;
  Restriction2: y - (40+5)*z <= 5;
  Objective:    x + y - z = MAX
end
```

The Declaration Section consists here of the reserved word **var** and an explicit list of all variable names. The Model Section, which includes the linear restrictions, begins with the reserved word **model** and ends with the reserved word **end**.

LPL language objects must be separated by at least one of the following delimiters: a blank, an end of line, or a comment.

The maximum length of a programming line is 130 characters. Beyond that limit all characters are ignored by the editor and compiler.

Each restriction must end with a semicolon. The objective function must include the reserved word **min** or **max**, which may be followed by a bracketed identifier.

3.3 INDEXED OBJECTS

3.3.1 Index-Sets

The need to group basic objects as variables, constraints or coefficients is a practical necessity in large linear programs. The analyst may for example not only define a variable 'Quantity', but a variable 'Quantity Q for several products p', or even 'Quantity Q for several products p produced in different periods t'. In mathematics this may be expressed by the notation Q_p or $Q_{p,t}$. These are variables with one or several subscripts - called *indices* or *sets* within LPL. A similar notation is used in LPL: A variable Q with the two indices p and t is written as 'Q(p,t)' or as 'Q[p,t]'. The indices are also identifiers and have the same syntax as variable identifiers. (To use more explicit identifiers, the LP modeler may also write 'Quantity[products,periods]').

The same is true for coefficients: A cost coefficient $c_{p,t}$ may be declared in LPL as 'c[p,t]' running through the indices 'p' and 't', where p∗t values are defined.

Constraints as well as variables or coefficients can be indexed. The same constraint 'R' can be applicable, for example, for all products 'p'. In LPL this fact is declared as 'R[p]'. Terms like 'Q[p,t]', 'c[p,t]' and 'R[p]' are called *indexed objects*.

3.3.2 Declaration of Index-Sets in LPL

Indices - like p and t - must be declared in an LPL program before they are used in indexed objects. Therefore, index- or *set declarations*, headed by the reserved word **set**, must be included at the beginning of the Declaration Section. The set declarations of 'p' and 't' containing, respectively, three and four items may be declared in LPL as follows:

```
SET
    p = (p1:p3)   { where 'p1:p3' is an abbreviation of 'p1  p2  p3' }
    t = (1:4)     { where '1:4' is an abbreviation of  '1  2  3  4' }
```

or with more explicit items:

```
    p = ( potatoes  corn  rye )
    t = ( FirstPeriod  SecondPeriod  ThirdPeriod  LastPeriod )
```

'p1', 'p2', etc. are called *items* or *elements* of the index-set 'p'. Items may be identifiers or numbers. They are either explicitly listed in a bracketed array, or written as two numbers, separated by a colon, which defines a range of integer items. A

12

subsequent variable declaration 'Q[p,t]' defines, as is shown in the example, 12 (=3*4) single variables: from 'Q[p1,1]' to 'Q[p3,4]'.

3.3.3 Declaration of Indexed Objects

Indexed objects as well as basic objects must be declared before they are used in the constraints.

All numerical values, coefficients and right-hand sides used in an LPL program, may be directly entered in a linear constraint as seen in example 'MODEL1.LPL'. LPL, however, also permits the modeler to assign numerical values to user-defined identifiers. These identifiers must be defined in the Declaration Section of an LPL program, namely in the *Coefficient Declaration Subsection*. This Subsection is headed by the reserved word **coef** and immediately follows the set declarations. Single, as well as indexed coefficients can be assigned:

```
COEF
  a = 3.5                          {single coefficient a and b}
  b = -34.786
  c[p] = ( 456   765   -89.9 )     {indexed coefficient c over index p}
  d[p,t] = ( 25   56.8   -6.7   9  {two dimensional indexed coefficient d}
             7     -     0.0   1
            34   -7.8   121   5 )
```

The numerical values within an indexed coefficient are listed in lexicographic (row major) order of the corresponding indices (see Knuth 1973, p.296). A nonexistent value is represented by a dash (-) or the real number, '-99.99'.

The variables are declared in the *Variable Declaration Subsection* headed by the reserved word **var** . As every model consists of at least one variable, the Variable Declaration Subsection must be present in all LPL programs. As in the Coefficient Declaration Subsection, single or structured variables, defined over several indices, are allowed.

EXAMPLES:

```
VAR
  x;        { a single variable, 'x' }
  Q(p,t);   { a two dimensional variable, 'Q' }
```

The constraint types are declared in the *Restriction Declaration Subsection* headed by the reserved word **res** .

13

EXAMPLE:

```
RES
   R(p)
```

This Subsection, however, is optional or may be replaced by the **forall** option in the Model Section (see below).

3.3.4 The SUM and FORALL Operators

The Sum and Forall Operators, used within the Model Section, act upon sets (indices). The SUM operator, invoked by the reserved word **sum**, is used to build sums over indexed variables or coefficients, like the sigma sign in arithmetic expressions. Thus mathematical terms like:

$$\sum_{p=1}^{3} Q_p \quad \text{or} \quad \sum_{p=1}^{3} \sum_{t=1}^{4} Q_{p,t}$$

may be expressed in LPL notation as,

```
SUM[p]  Q[p]     or     SUM[p,t]  Q[p,t]
```

The FORALL operator, invoked by the reserved word **forall**, is used in a similar fashion, but applies to constraints. It allows the modeler to summarize several constraints in a single restriction. A construction like:

Restriction i : . . . . .   where i = { 1, ... ,n}

will be expressed in LPL as,

```
Restriction : FORALL[i]  .....
```

where 'Restriction' is the name of the constraint chosen by the user and 'i' must have been previously declared as an index. The FORALL operator may be dropped, if the indexed identifier 'Restriction[i]' was declared as a restriction. This declaration takes place in the Declaration Section headed by the reserved word **res**.

14

3.4 OVERVIEW OF THE DESIGN OF AN LPL PROGRAM

An LPL program consists, in the following order of a:

> Heading Section   (optional)
> Declaration Section
> Model Section.

The Declaration Section and Model Section may be repeated several times.

3.4.1 The Heading Section

In LPL, the program heading is purely optional and has no significance to the program itself. If present, it gives the program a name, which is treated as a comment. It consists of the reserved word **program** followed by an identifier and a semicolon.

3.4.2 The Declaration Section

The Declaration Section defines all the identifiers which will be used within the Model Section. It is divided into four subsections listed below in the prescribed order:

> Set Declaration Subsection
> Coefficient Declaration Subsection
> Variable Declaration Subsection (obligatory)
> Restriction Declaration Subsection (optional)

They have already been described above.

3.4.3 The Model Section

The whole structure of the LP model is defined in the Model Section. In LPL, each linear restriction or type of linear restriction, (the restrictions, as well as the objective function), can be written in a form similar to mathematical notation. The Model Section is headed be the reserved word **model** and ended by the reserved word **end**. Between these two reserved words the linear equations are listed and separated by a semicolon. Each constraint type may be named by an identifier, or by any string enclosed in apostrophes. This name must be placed at the beginning of a constraint followed by a colon.

EXAMPLE:

```
model
  R:  x + 5*y = 6*z - 8;
  '2-4':  (6+5)*x + (a*b+c)*y = d;
  Res_Type:  forall(i)  x - sum(j) (a[i,j]*y[j,i] + a*z[i] +c) = 18
     { where 'i' and 'j' are sets, 'a' and 'c' are coefficients and }
     { 'x','y','z' are model variables;
        'R','2-4' and 'Res_Type' are constraint names }
  end
```

A whole LPL program looks like:

```
PROGRAM program_name;  {optional}
SET
  { indices are declared here }
COEF
  { the data are declared here }
VAR
  { variables declaration }
RES
  { constraint types declaration }
MODEL
  { the constraints written in algebraic notation }
END
```

The general LP model defined above in matrix notation can, therefore, be formulated in LPL as follows:

Primal problem:

```
SET
  i = (1:m)  {where 'm' is an integer}
  j = (1:n)  {where 'n' is an integer}
COEF
  A[i,j] = ( {insert n*m data} )
  b[i]   = ( {insert m data} )
  c[j]   = ( {insert n data} )
VAR
  x[j]
RES
  r[i]
MODEL
  r: sum(i)  A*x = b;
     c*x = MAX
END
```

Dual problem:

```
SET
  i = (1:m)
  j = (1:n)
COEF
  A[i,j] = ( {n*m data} )
  b[i]   = ( {m data} )
  c[j]   = ( {n data} )
VAR
  r[i]
RES
  x[j]
MODEL
  x: sum(j)  A*r = c;
     b*r = MIN
END
```

Note that indices may be omitted in the constraints in order to make the expressions more readable. To switch between the primal and the dual formulation, only the vectors **b** and **c**, and **x** and **r** need be exchanged.

The following LP model shows a complete formulation of a transportation problem in LPL notation:

```
(* SHIP0.LPL: a simple transportation problem
   Problem: Goods must be shipped from 10 production
   centers to 6 distribution centers with minimal costs
(*****************************************************)
{$Cv(1,2)+i1(1,2)+i2(1,2)   this is a compiler directive}
Set
   i = (1:10)        {supplier}
   j = (1:6)         {demander}
Coef
   { Transportation costs from i to j }
   costs[i,j]  =    ( 5    4    6    7    8   4.5
                     10    0   12   23    5   6.5
                     11    8   13   17    2   7.8
                      5    5   10   34   10   4
                     18    0    0   11   17   2.3
                      7    9    9   34   23   9.9
                     12   10   14    -    8   2
                      4   77   11    -    9   1
                     16   16   12    8   12   5.6
                     23   67    2   12    4   7.7)
   { (maximum) quantities supplied at i }
   supply[i]   =    (134 120 301 400 290 398 678 456 1729 456)
   { (minimal) quantities demanded at j }
   demand[j]   =    (923 45 78.98 300 589 678)
Var
   QUANTITY[i,j]   {unknown quantity to transport from i to j}

Model
   SUPPLIES : forall[i]   sum[j]  QUANTITY <= supply;
   DEMANDS  : forall[j]   sum[i]  QUANTITY >= demand;
   OBJECTIVE: sum[i,j]  costs * QUANTITY = min(cost)
End
```

3.5 SUBSET SELECTIONS

Each index contains a declared list of items, as shown above. There are different possibilities to select, extract or total any subset of that list. Like subscripted algebraic expressions in mathematics, indices in LPL may be exchanged or replaced by other indices. They may even be used within arithmetic expressions. Different examples may clarify these powerful expressions. Suppose for instance, that the following indices and variable have been declared:

```
SET
  p  = ( potatoes  corn  rye )
  t  = ( FirstPeriod  SecondPeriod  ThirdPeriod  LastPeriod )
  p1 = ( rye  potatoes )
  t1 = ( FirstPeriod  LastPeriod )
VAR
  Q[p,t]
  .....
```

With Q[p,t], 12 single variables have been declared: Q[potatoes,FirstPeriod] ...
Q[rye,LastPeriod]. Different expressions may be used in a subsequent Model Section:

With SUM[p,t] Q[p,t]   or   SUM[p,t] Q   or   SUM[p,t] Q[,] ,
all 12 variables are totaled. (Indices may be dropped).

With SUM[t] Q[potatoes,t]   or   SUM[t] Q[potatoes,] ,
the corresponding variables are totaled over the four periods.

With SUM[p1,t1] Q[p1,t1]   or   SUM[p1,t1] Q ,
summation extends over p1 and t1 and only the four corresponding variables are
extracted and totaled.

With SUM[p,t] Q[p1,t1] ,
summation extends over p and t, but only the four variables corresponding to the
indices p1 and t1 are extracted and totaled.

With SUM[p,t] Q[t,p] ,
nothing will be totaled, since p and t have no common item. (If p and t were to have
common items, summation would extend over the common items only).

With ... + Q[potatoes+1,LastPeriod-1] + ...,
the variable Q[corn,ThirdPeriod] is added.

With SUM[p,t] Q[p+1,2*t] ,
summation extends over p and t, but only terms beginning at the second period (p+1) in
combination with each second product (2*p) will be extracted.

All extractions may also be combined with the FORALL operator.

To show the resemblance between LPL notation and normal algebraic notation,
consider the following production model:

"A company manufactures three products P1, P2, P3 and has at its disposal three machines M1, M2, M3. The company can undertake normal and overtime production and needs to plan for two time periods, say WINTER and SUMMER. Any product left after the second time period has a very small resale value. ... It is necessary to find an LP formulation that maximizes the profit of the company's operation over the two periods." (Ellison 1982, p.238).

This is the LPL representation of the model for this problem:

```
(* PRODUCT1.LPL: a simple production model.
(*****************************************)
{$Cv(1,1)+i1(1,1)+i2(1,1)+i3(1,1)+i4(1,1)   compiler directive}
Set
    i = (1:2)          { Time period: summer and winter }
    j = (1:2)          { Modes of production: normal,overtime }
    k = (1:3)          { Index for the product types: P1,P2,P3 }
    l = (1:3)          { Index for the machines: M1,M2,M3 }

Coef
    t(i,j,k,l) = (4 7 3   5 6 -   6 6 -    {Table of machine hours}
                  3 6 2   4 5 -   5 5 -
                  5 8 4   6 7 -   7 7 -
                  4 7 3   5 6 -   5 6 -)
    c(i,j,k,l) = (2 4 1   3 3 -   4 2 -    {the production cost}
                  3 5 2   4 4 -   5 3 -
                  3 5 2   4 4 -   5 3 -
                  4 6 3   5 5 -   6 4 -)
    a(i,j,l)   = (100 100 40   80  90 30   {machine availability}
                  110 110 50   90 100 40)
    p(i,k)     = (10 10  9   11 11 10)      {selling price}
    d(i,k)     = (25 30 30   30 25 25)      {demand}
    s(k)       = ( 1   1   1 )              {storage cost}
    h(k)       = (20  20   - )              {storage capacity}
    r(k)       = ( 2   2   1 )              {final resale value}

Var
    X like t    {the quantity of product to be produced see below}
    Y(i,k)      {the quantity of product to be stored}
    Z(i,k)      {the quantity of product k sold in the period i }

Model
    (* the profit function: *)
    sum(i,j,k,l) (p-c)*X - sum(k) (s*Y[1,] + (r-p[2,])*Y[2,]) = MAX(profit);
    (* constraints of machine availability: *)
    MACHINES: forall(i,j,l)  sum(k) t * X  <= a;
    (* stock balances in the two periods *)
    STOCK1: forall(k) sum(j,l) X[1,,,] - Y[1,] - Z[1,] = 0;
    STOCK2: forall(k) sum(j,l) X[2,,,] + Y[1,] - Y[2,] - Z[2,] = 0;
    (* minimum demands to be satisfied *)
    DEMAND: forall(i,k)  Z  >=  d;
    (* upper bound on storage *)
    BOUND: forall(k)  Y[1,]  <=  h
end
```

This model was used by Ellison to illustrate the MGG modeling language. The same model written in LPL, with more explicit identifiers is found in Appendix 2, with the name 'PRODUCT.LPL'.

In the Variable Declaration of the last LPL model, the expression 'X **like** t' has been used. **like** is a reserved word of the LPL language, and means that the variable 'X' has the same index-list as the coefficient 't'. Furthermore, the single variable within 'X' corresponds to a nonexistent coefficient, and thus, cannot be used in the Model Section. The consequence of this kind of Variable Declaration is that the number of variables may not only be dependent on the sets, but also on the data in an LP model. This produces a very useful effect.

3.6 HIERARCHICAL INDEX-SETS

The LPL language would be very limited with only the above mentioned features. In this section advanced features are discussed.

3.6.1 Definition of an Hierarchical Structure (Tree):
An index-set in LPL may be a more complex entity than just a linear list of different items such as numbers and identifiers. It can be built as an hierarchical, recursive structure which is represented by a *tree*.
A tree is written as an hierarchical list as follows:

        A = (B (E (J K) F) C (G) D (H (L) I))

This list may also be represented by a tree, as shown in Fig. 3-1.

'A' is called the *root*; items other than the root which have descendants are called *sub-indices* or *subsets*; these descendants are called *sons*. So 'E' and 'F' are the sons of the subset 'B'. Items with no descendants are called *leaves* ('J','K','I' ect.).

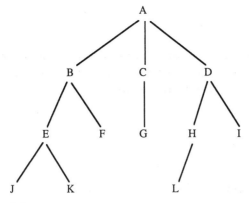

Fig. 3-1.

3.6.2 Notation in LPL

An hierarchical list may be presented in LPL as shown below:

```
SET
 A = ( B ( E ( J K ) F ) C ( G ) D ( H ( L ) I ) )
```

And yet since LPL has a free format this same set may also be written as:

```
SET
 A = ( B
        ( E ( J  K )
          F
        )
        C ( G )
        D ( H ( L )
            I
          )
      )
```

or in any other desired arrangement.

3.6.3 An Example

Suppose we were to build an LP model concerned with agriculture and we want to define a variable called 'ProductSurface', which indicates the (unknown) surfaces of different crops. 'ProductSurface' may be indexed by 'Surfaces' and declared as follows:

```
VAR
   ProductSurface (Surfaces);
```

'Surfaces', is an index within LPL and may by divided into 'mountain' and 'plain', and
these divisions may be further subdivided into other subsurfaces and so on. In LPL this
hierarchical structure may be declared as follows:

```
SET
   Surfaces =
      (Mountain
         (Alpine Crops
            (Root_Crop  (Vegetables Potatoes)
            Forage_Crop (Summer_Barley Oat)
            Bread_Crop  (Winter_Wheat Summer_Wheat Rye)
            )
         )
      Plain
         (Meadow Crops
            (Root_Crop  (Corn Vegetables Potatoes Sugar_Beet Beans)
            Forage_Crop (Summer_Barley Winter_Barley Oat )
            Bread_Crop  (Winter_Wheat Summer_Wheat Rye)
            )
         )
      )
```

Since the same identifier may have multiple occurrences within an hierarchical index-
set, there must exist a distinguishing characteristic. This is given by a notation called
path. 'Oat' for instance occurs within 'mountain' and 'plain', and is distinguished by
the paths 'Mountain:Oat' and 'Plain:Oat'. Hence, in the Model Section (within the
restrictions) expressions like:

```
... + sum[Plain] ProductSurface (Plain) + ...
...forall[crops] ProductSurface (Mountain:crops) ...
...+ ProductSurface (Plain:Oat) + ...
```

may be used to denote a part or a single variable of 'ProductSurface'.

3.6.4 Consequences on the Operators

This structuring of index-sets has important consequences on the SUM and FORALL
operators. It may be necessary to run through sets in different ways. Index names
preceded by the signs '&', '#' and '*' are used in the Model Section to tell the SUM or
FORALL operator how to run through the indices. To explain this mechanism, consider
the following set declaration:

22

```
SET
    A = ( B ( E ( J K ) F ) C ( G ) D ( H ( L ) I ) )
```

In the Model Section different expressions may be used:

```
.. SUM(A) ...   means   'run through the sons of A only'  (B, C and D)
.. SUM(&A) ...  means   'run through the leaves of A'  (J, K, F, G, L and I)
.. SUM(&#A) ... means   'run through all items of A'
.. SUM(#A)  ... means   'run through all subset items of A'  (B, E, C, D and H)
```

Of course, the first three terms are identical, if all sons of the index 'A' are leaves or, in other words, if 'A' represents a linear list of items. In a similar way, different selections of restrictions may be obtained with the FORALL operator.

The symbol '*' is used in a special context, where the symbol '#' had been used before in a FORALL expression of the same restriction.

EXAMPLE:
consider the restriction:

```
forall[#A] .... + sum[*A] x + ... = + ... + x + ....
```

where 'x' is a variable declared as 'x[A]'.
'*A' is said to be bounded to '#A', while '#A' runs through the elements B, E, C, D and H, *A runs through *their* sons. This means:

if #A has reached B, *A runs through E and F
if #A has reached E, *A runs through J and K
if #A has reached C, *A runs through G
if #A has reached D, *A runs through H and I
if #A has reached H, *A runs through L

This means that this restriction type will produce the five following constraints:

```
..... + x[E] + x[F] + ... = ... + x[B] + ....
..... + x[J] + x[K] + ... = ... + x[E] + ....
..... + x[G] + ...        = ... + x[C] + ....
..... + x[H] + x[I] + ... = ... + x[D] + ....
..... + x[L] + ...        = ... + x[H] + ....
```

This permits the modeler to define hierarchical restriction structures according to the hierarchical set structure.

3.7 INTERFACES TO DATABASES

Large LP models generally have a great deal of data (coefficients). It would be almost impossible or at least an enormous waste of effort, to place all the data within an LPL program. Often all the data are already stored in databases. For this reason, LPL offers an integrated interface with the popular software packages dBASEII and dBASEIII. dBASE is a relational database system, where files are organized into columns (the fields) and rows (the records). The fields can contain alpha-numerical or numerical information. A typical small database, called 'ANIMALS', is shown in Table 3-1.

FIELDS:	ANIMAL	GROUP	NUMBER	PRICE	GROWTH
RECORD1:	cows	cattle	2070	900.25	+120.05
RECORD2:	bulls	cattle	700	967.50	+17.6
RECORD3:	oxen	cattle	60	409.00	−50
RECORD4:	rabbits	rodents	679	3.89	+786
RECORD5:	hens and cocks	poultry	34987	1.40	+123.8
RECORD6:	turkeys	poultry	5678	1.80	−3.3
RECORD7:	beavers	rodents	8	99.05	−567

TABLE 3-1.

'ANIMAL' and 'GROUP' are fieldnames of alpha-numeric fields, 'NUMBER' 'PRICE' and 'GROWTH' are fieldnames of numeric fields. The whole database contains seven records. This is all that an LPL programmer must know about the database! For more information refer to the dBASE manuals (Ashton-Tate 1985).

The interface with databases in LPL has three aspects:
- transferring a list of items to a set declaration directly from a database.
- reading numerical values from a database.
- creating empty but structured database files, setting all data to '-99.99' (the nonexistent data).

3.7.1 The LongList Option

Sometimes it is convenient to input a whole array of identifiers already defined in a database and to declare the array as a set.

The following instruction within LPL transfers the list of animals from the first field of the database 'ANIMALS' and assigns them to the set 'animals':

```
animals = filetable 'ANIMALS' 1
```

where 'animals' is the name of the set within LPL, **filetable** is a reserved word and indicates that the elements should be read from the database and 'ANIMALS' is the filename of the database file. The filename must be enclosed in apostrophes. (It is not necessary to append the filename extension.) The last number '1' is the field number where the elements can be found. Since a dBASE file allows any string in an alpha-numeric field, this contradicts the element identifier syntax within LPL. Thus, LPL must translate the alpha-numeric string into a conforming LPL identifier syntax. The rule of this translation is very simple: all special characters, (i.e. blanks), are eliminated. Thus, the string 'hens and cocks' will be translated into 'hensandcocks'. Such translations, however, could be avoided by the appropriate choice of a string in the database. 'hens_and_cocks' or 'hens_cocks', for example, would not need to be changed.

Note, however, that since identifiers within LPL are limited in length to 15 significant characters, the remaining characters will be truncated.

There is yet another possibility for reading items from a database file and for producing hierarchical sets. Suppose that the goal is to define the following hierarchical set according to the database 'ANIMALS':

```
SET
   animals=(cattle   (cows bulls oxen)
            poultry (HensAndCocks turkeys)
            rodents (rabbits beavers)
           )
```

For an extensive database, it would be an enormous waste of effort to copy all the sets and subsets into an LPL program. LPL provides a solution to this problem. The following set declaration will have the same effect as the explicit set definition above:

```
animals = filetable 'ANIMALS' 2 1
```

Here '2 1' means that the elements are all found in the first field, and that the second field is used to build subset names and to produce the different subsets. LPL automatically produces as many different subsets as there are corresponding items in field 2, the elements of which are found in field 1. Duplicate elements in a subset are not allowed and the compiler will automatically detect them.

3.7.2 Reading Data from Databases

If a great deal of data is to be assigned to a multidimensional coefficient, it would be cumbersome to enter all the data in an LPL program. Furthermore, if the sets used as indices contain subsets, it would be almost impossible for the programmer to have complete control of the element order and therefore, impossible for him to write the data in the correct place within an LPL program. The compiler provides only minimal control, through the numbers of data items. If a wrong number of data has been assigned to an indexed coefficient, the compiler detects it and stops with an error message.

To avoid these difficulties, LPL provides another interface to the database, dBASE, in order to read the correct data at compilation time.

To illustrate this powerful tool, the transportation problem 'SHIP0.LPL' used in Chapter 3.4 is reformulated below, where all the data are stored in a database 'SHIP1'. This database has the structure exposed in TABLE 3-2.

FLDS: From/To	Zurich	Geneva	Lausanne	Fribourg	Basel	Sion	Supply
Rotterdam	5.0	4.0	6.0	7.00	8.0	4.5	134
Berlin	10.0	0.0	12.0	23.00	5.0	6.5	120
Amsterdam	11.0	8.0	13.0	17.00	2.0	7.8	301
New_York	5.0	5.0	10.0	34.00	10.0	4.0	400
Paris	18.0	0.0	0.0	11.00	17.0	2.3	290
Madrid	7.0	9.0	9.0	34.00	23.0	9.9	398
Moscow	12.0	10.0	14.0	-99.99	8.0	2.0	678
London	4.0	77.0	11.0	-99.99	9.0	1.0	456
Peking	16.0	16.0	12.0	8.00	12.0	5.6	1729
Tokyo	23.0	67.0	2.0	12.00	4.0	7.7	456
Demand	923.0	45.0	78.9	300.00	589.0	678.0	0

TABLE 3-2.

All numerical values in the database 'SHIP1' can be read with the following LPL instruction:

```
Coef
    table(i,j)  =  filetable 'SHIP1'
```

where 'table' is the coefficient name within LPL, 'i' and 'j' are the indices of this coefficient, **filetable** is a reserved word and 'SHIP1' is the name of the database. The indices 'i' and 'j' may or may not have been declared in a preceding Set Declaration Subsection. If they have not been declared, they are automatically produced by this instruction, as follows: The elements in the first field ('Rotterdam' . . . 'Demand') are assigned to the index 'i' and the fieldnames, except for the first one, ('Zurich' . . .

'Supply') are assigned to the index 'j'. Therefore, the instruction will not only transfer all the necessary data, but will also implicitly produce two sets, 'i' and 'j'.

If the sets 'i' or 'j' had already been declared in an LPL program, only the corresponding fields and records would have been transferred from the database. Thus, the instructions:

```
SET
   i = (Rotterdam Amsterdam New_York)
   j = (Zurich Fribourg Sion Lausanne)
COEF
   table(i,j) = filetable 'SHIP1'
```

would only assign the 12 corresponding data to the coefficient 'table', leaving the indices 'i' and 'j' unchanged.

The whole transportation problem may now be concisely formulated in LPL as:

```
(* SHIP1.LPL: the same as 'SHIP0.LPL' *)
Program Transportation;
     {$Ci1(1,3)+'.'+i2(1,3)   = instruction for column names}
Coef  table(i,j)  =  filetable 'SHIP1'  { data table }
Var   QUANTITY like table               { unknown quantity }
Res   SUPPLIES(i)   DEMANDS(j)          { restriction types }

Model
  SUPPLIES : sum(j) QUANTITY[i- 1,j- 1] <= table[i- 1,supply];
  DEMANDS  : sum(i) QUANTITY[i- 1,j- 1] >= table[demand,j- 1];
  OBJECTIVE: sum(i,j) table[i- 1,j- 1] * QUANTITY[i- 1,j- 1] = MIN
end
```

Note that the vastness of the transportation problem is no longer visible in this formulation, depending solely on the size of the database file 'SHIP1'!

One reservation, however, exists while reading data from a database: the coefficient 'table' must have exactly two indices, here 'i' and 'j', any additional indices would produce a compilation error.

3.7.3 Creating an Empty Database

It may, occasionally, be reasonable to build an LP, even if the data are not yet available. A special command within LPL creates empty but structured database files setting all data to '-99.99' (the nonexistent data value), which may then be filled-up later on. The following LPL instructions accomplish this task:

27

```
SET
    i= (Rotterdam Berlin Amsterdam New_York Paris Madrid Moscow London
        Peking Tokyo Demand)
    j= (Zurich Geneva Lausanne Fribourg Basel Sion Supply)
COEF
    table(i,j) = maketable 'SHIP1'
```

The reserved word **filetable** is replaced by **maketable**. The main menu (see Chapter 5.2.) of LPL includes an option 'create empty dBase' (command **B**), which produces the same database file 'SHIP1' as in Section 3.7.2. but with all numeric values set to '-99.99'. If the file 'SHIP1' already exists, the message 'overwrite? (Y/N)' is printed on the screen and the modeler may enter his answer.

At compilation time the whole database is read exactly in the same way as above.

Note that the structure of a dBASE file created by the selection **B** must not be changed, otherwise the LPL compiler will not be able to read the file.

3.8 ADDITIONAL LANGUAGE ELEMENTS

There exist additional language elements which are particularly interesting for large LP problems. The nomenclature problem, mentioned in Chapter 2, is always a tricky question. On the one hand, unique row- and column-names should be produced, and on the other hand, most LP solution packages accept only eight characters to build these names. LPL provides a solution to this problem through user-controlled names for rows and columns and alias names for items. Another common problem involves organizing the structure of large models. LPL provides the possibility for defining submodels.

3.8.1 Alias Names of Items

After each element in a Set Declaration Subsection, a unique alias name may be added, enclosed in apostrophes.

EXAMPLE:

```
SET
    products = ( beans'P1' crop'P2' rye'P3' )
```

'P1' is an alias name for 'beans', 'P2' for 'crop', etc. The alias name may contain any characters, but it must not exceed 3 characters. The unique use of this alias name is for controlling the entire production of the internal row- and column-names, (see user controlled row- and column-names in Chapter 3.8.2).

3.8.2 User-Controlled Row and Column-Names

In an LPL program, any identifier up to 15 characters long may be a variable name. This variable name is called the *external name*. Since MPSX, for example, accepts variable names up to 8 characters only, the LPL nomenclature must be translated by the LPL compiler into a text string called the *internal name*, which must not exceed this 8 characters limit in order to respect this MPSX restriction. Furthermore, this translation must produce a unique name for each row and column, otherwise the names get confused. This translation in LPL is carried out as follows:

The first three (or less) characters are taken from the external variable identifier defined in the LPL program. All variables are numbered by the compiler in the order in which they occur in the LPL program and this unique number is appended to the three characters. Indexed variables have in their internal notations, the same three leading characters to which a unique number produced by the compiler is added. This guarantees a unique internal variable name for each single variable used in an LP program.

The restriction names are produced in the same manner. Three (or less) characters head the string of the internal restriction name. The three characters are taken from the optional restriction name or the restriction identifier defined in the Declaration Section within the LPL program and a unique number is added to the string. If no name has been given to the restriction the three letter heading, 'RES', is generated.

Unfortunately, this mechanism may produce unreadable row- and column-names for large LP's. LPL provides, therefore, for user-controlled production of these names. The specification of the internal row- and column-names must be included within an LPL program as a special comment (beginning with '{' or '(*'). This comment is called a *compiler directive*. It may be put anywhere, like the comment before the Model Section. A dollar sign must immediately follow the '{' or '(*'. The next character in the compiler directive is a 'C' or an 'R' depending on whether the directive is valid for column- or row-names. Thus, the beginning strings of a compiler directive are:

    {$C....   or (*$C.... for column names

    {$R....   or (*$R.... for row names.

This heading string is followed by up to 7 components separated by an addition sign. The internal names are composed in the order of the different components. Five different type of components are distinguished, each headed by one of the five characters: 'v', 'i', 'a', ''' (an apostrophe) or 'n'.

The *v type* means that the characters must be extracted from the external name. To extract characters it is necessary to indicate the positions of the characters to extract.

29

This is accomplished by two numbers separated by a comma and enclosed in brackets. Example: The component 'v(2,3)' means that the second, third and fourth characters are extracted from the external name and added to the internal name.

The *i type* means that the characters must be extracted from a corresponding element. Example: The component i3(1,2) means that the first two characters are extracted from the corresponding element of the third index of the variable or constraint name. If the variable or constraint has less the three indices, nothing will be extracted.

The *a type* does the same as the i type, but the alias name of the element is considered. Example: The component a2 means that the corresponding alias name is extracted from the second index.

The *' (apostrophe) type* adds any string specified within apostrophes to the internal row- or column-name. Example: The component '.' adds a point to the internal name. Up to 5 characters may be added within apostrophes.

The *n type* adds a unique number produced by the compiler to the internal name.

The syntax of the compiler directive is very strict. No blank or other characters must be included, otherwise the compiler directive will be interpreted as an ordinary comment.

Some compiler directive examples may serve to clarify this syntax:

- {$Cv(1,2)+'-'+a1+'-'+i2(1,3) compiler directive for column names}

The internal variable name is composed of 5 components. The first two characters are extracted from the variable identifier. This is extended by a dash (-). The alias name is now appended from the first index followed by another dash, and the string is terminated by the first three characters of the corresponding element of the second index.

- {$Ci1(3,1)+'.'+v(1,3)+n this is another compiler directive}

The third character is extracted from the corresponding element of the first index. This is extended by a point. Then the first three characters are appended from the variable identifier. The string is terminated by a unique number produced by the compiler.

- {$Cv(1,3)+n this is the default compiler directive}

The last compiler directive is the default as explained above.

By this means, the LPL modeler may build his own internal variable and restriction names in a complex way. But he should by aware of two things: 1) the internal variable name cannot exceed 8 characters according to the MPSX Standard, and 2) several variables may consist of the same string rendering them undistinguishable by MPSX. Thus, the LP modeler should carefully plan his internal definitions.

The default compiler directive always produces unique internal names for each variable and constraint declared in the LPL program, since a unique number, 'n', produced by the compiler is added at the end.

3.8.3 Data in the Set Declaration

Some data may be assigned directly in the Set Declaration Subsection. This is particularly useful if one-dimensional coefficients are used. The following is an example:

```
set
  i = (t  u  v  w  x  y  z);
coef
  a(i) = (  -  1  2.4  -6.7  8  -  -  )
  b(i) = (  2  -  -23  5.56  -  -  8  )
  c(i) = (  1  0  -  10.3  -  -  -  )
```

'a', 'b' and 'c' are three coefficients running through the index 'i'. They may be directly assigned in the Set Declaration Subsection as follows:

```
Set
  i/a/b/c = ( t/-/2/1   u/1/-/0   v/2.4/-23/-   w/-6.7/5.56/10.3   x/8/-/-
              y   z/-/8/-
            )
```

The data directly follow the corresponding element separated by slashes (/), in the order of the coefficient identifiers, which must follow the set identifier and are separated by slashes. The number of data after each element must correspond to the number of coefficient identifiers or no data may follow (see 'y' in the last example). No data following the element means that the corresponding values are nonexistent.

If any alias name is used, the data must *follow* the alias name.

Two simple LP models called 'ROBOT.LPL' and 'ROBOT1.LPL' serve to demonstrate the advantages of this kind of declaration. 'ROBOT.LPL' is formulated as follows:

31

```
(* ROBOT.LPL: A firm produces two type of robots called 'Marie' and 'Jules'.
   Three production steps must be carried out:
   - Production of the components, which takes 5 hours for each robot
     Marie and Jules, with a total capacity of 350 hours per week;
   - mounting (capacity=480) taking 4 hours for Marie and 8 hours for Jules
   - testing (capacity=300) taking 6 hours for Marie and 2 hours for Jules.
   The selling prices for Marie is $300 and for Jules $200.
   There are already 20 Marie's and 15 Jules' ordered.
   How many robots of each type can be produced per week, if the
   firm wants to maximize the selling profit? *)
 (*************************************************************************)
 {$Cv(1,5)  this is the compiler directive}

 var
   Marie Jules

 model
   Production_Step:     5*Marie + 5*Jules  <=  350;
   Mounting_Step:       4*Marie + 8*Jules  <=  480;
   Test_Step:           6*Marie + 2*Jules  <=  300;
   Ordered_Marie:       Marie >= 20;        {Minimal Number to produce}
   Ordered_Jules:       Jules >= 15;        {Minimal Number to produce}
   Objective_function: 300*Marie + 200*Jules = Max(profit);
 end.
```

Another more general formulation of this problem, as shown in 'ROBOT1.LPL', is:

```
(* ROBOT1.LPL: This is another, more general LPL formulation of the model
   'ROBOT.LPL' *)
 {$Ci1(1,5)  this is the compiler directive}
 Set
   robots/price/Ordered = ( Marie/300/20   Jules/200/15 )
   ProductionSteps/Capacity {in hours per week}
        = ( Production/350  Mounting/480  Testing/300 )
 coef
   TimeCosts(Robots,ProductionSteps) = ( 5 4 6   5 8 2 )
 var
   Number(robots)

 model
   Production: forall(ProductionSteps) sum(robots)  TimeCosts*Number <=
 Capacity;
   Orders: forall(robots)  Number >= Ordered;
   MaximalProfit: sum(robots)  price*Number = MAX
 end
```

The greatest advantage of the second formulation is that an extension of the model (more production steps or more robot types) influences only the Declaration Section.

3.8.4 Sub-Models

In large LP models it may be helpful to subdivide the whole model into smaller units. In LPL, Declaration Sections and Model Sections may be repeated as many times as the modeler deems necessary. The following is a correct LPL formulation:

```
{first submodel}
SET
    .....
VAR
    ...
MODEL
    ...
{second submodel}
SET
    ...
COEF
    ...
MODEL
    ...
{other submodels can be added here}

{last submodel}
COEF
    ...
RES
    ...
MODEL
    ...
END
```

where preceding Declaration Sections have been used in a subsequent Model Section. No duplicate sets or coefficient, variable and restriction identifiers, however, are allowed in the different Sub-Models. The Sub-Model option is particulary useful, if the modeler works with large models. The entire model may be subdivided into logical sub-units. The modeler, however, should note that all declared identifiers are global definitions; there is no possibility of local declaration in a specified Sub-Model. A model is compiled until the reserved word **end** is found. The model 'EP.LPL' in Appendix 3 shows, how this powerful option may be used in real live modeling.

Chapter 4

The LPN Network

LPN (Linear Programming Network) was first introduced by Egli (Egli 1980) to document a specific, large LP model. This model, called EP model, is a long life model which has been under constant modification and adaptation for the last ten years. Without any doubt, we can say that the research group working with the EP model today, would not be able to understand the model without the LPN representation. This situation reveals another difficulty in working with large LP's. Continuing work with a large LP demands tools which make the model understandable to a changing crew at overall low costs. LPN has proved to be a particularly useful tool in allowing a continuous understanding of the structure of the EP model. Although LPN was initially conceived to document the EP model, it can be used for other LP models as well.

Like LPL, LPN expresses a complete LP model in symbolic form. LPN's basic and indexed objects are graphical tokens (squares, circles, lines etc.), rather then identifiers and real numbers. Rules prescribe the puzzle-like way in which these tokens must be put together. A graphical representation of a model generally gives more insight into its structure than algebraic notation. This chapter first defines the LPN objects and the rules for combining them. In order to be more general and systematic, the definition proposed in this chapter does not entirely correspond to the notation used by Egli. Some examples will then be used to illustrate the 'syntax' of LPN. The chapter ends with some remarks regarding the use of LPN as an analytical tool. Selected parts of the above mentioned EP model may be found in Appendix 3 in LPL notation.

4.2 BASIC AND INDEXED OBJECTS

The objects, basic as well as indexed, of an LP model (variables, constraints, right-hand sides, data and the objective function) are represented in LPN as graphical tokens, all of which find their counter-parts in the LPL syntax. Considering the same identifiers as in the matrix notation in FORMULAS 2-1 to 2-3, the corresponding objects in LPN are:

The square: | y | or | x_j | with j = {1...n}

representing a variable 'y' or an indexed variable 'x'.
If the variables are bounded at 1<=y<=u (lj<=xj<=uj), a double line on top or at the bottom is added. A lower bound of zero is not represented.

The circle: $(r_1 =)$ or $(r_i =)$ with i = {1...m}

representing a constraint r1 or a constraint type 'r' with the operator '='.

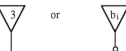

The triangle with an ending line at the bottom: (3)   or   (b_i)

representing a single right-hand side with the value '3' or a subscripted right-hand side vector 'b'.

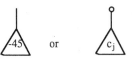

The pyramid with an ending line on top: (-45)   or   (c_j)

representing a value '-45' in the objective function or the cost vector in the objective function with their data 'c'.

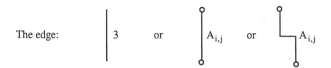

The edge: | 3   or | $A_{i,j}$ or $A_{i,j}$

representing the coefficient '3' in the matrix or data in the matrix $A_{i,j}$.

If the data **A**, **b** and **c** are indexed, the lines end with a small circle. These circles are called *selectors*, and their meaning is explained in Chapter 4.3.

Three rules prescribe how the different token should be linked together:

36

1) A triangle is always linked to a circle expressing that the corresponding constraints have right-hand sides. This is shown by Fig. 4-1. The way in which they are linked is not important.

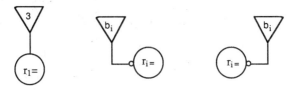

Fig. 4-1.

2) A pyramid is always linked to a square meaning that the corresponding variable is found in the objective function (see Fig. 4-2).

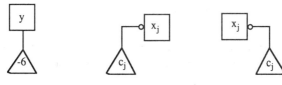

FIG. 4-2.

3) An edge links a circle with a square, if the variable occurs in the corresponding constraint or if the corresponding matrix element within A is different from zero. The edge must join a square on top or at the bottom depending on whether the sign of the variable in the corresponding constraint is negative or positive. Fig. 4-3 shows five possibilities of such edges. Circles may be joined anywhere by edges.

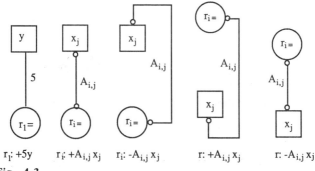

$r_i: +5y$ $r_i: +A_{i,j}x_j$ $r_i: -A_{i,j}x_j$ $r: +A_{i,j}x_j$ $r: -A_{i,j}x_j$

Fig. 4-3.

These three rules form an integral part of the LPN syntax. With the exception of these rules, the modeler is free to arrange the objects as he desires. The two following constraints:

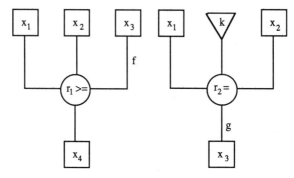

Fig. 4-4a and 4-4b.

The general LP, as previously defined in matrix notation (FORMULA 2-1 to 2-4), is translated below into an LPN formulation. (Fig. 4-5a and 4-5b).

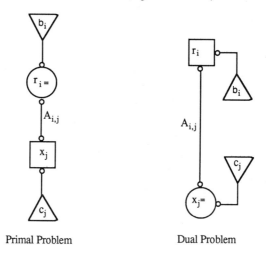

Primal Problem   Dual Problem

Fig. 4-5a and 4-5b.

The above LPN formulation is the most abstract representation of an LP model. It does not express a concrete LP problem. All the objects necessary to define a complete LP, however, are present: the square representing the variable vector x; the circle representing the constraint vector r; and the triangle, the pyramid and the edge

38

representing the data **b**, **c** and **A**. As was the case with LPL notation, the primal and dual LPN formulations are symmetrical. Triangles are exchanged against pyramids; circles against squares and vice versa to pass from one problem to the other. These are very important properties of the LPN formulation.

In order to learn to design a concrete LP problem, Fig. 4-6 shows the simple model, 'MODEL1.LPL', previously defined in Chapter 3, in an LPN formulation.

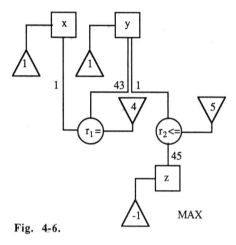

Fig. 4-6.

The right-hand side and the cost vector data are directly assigned to the triangles and pyramids. No difference is made between positive and negative values. The sign of a coefficient in the matrix **A**, however, expresses some structural information and may, therefore, affect the design. The coefficient, (i.e. '45'), has a negative sign in the constraint r_2, but is represented in LPN as a positive value. This negativity is expressed by the fact that 'z' is joined on the top. Formally, the variable could be joined at the bottom, but in this case the coefficient should have been represented as a negative number. A concrete representation of an LPN problem depends largely upon the manner in which the modeler decides to interpret his model. The only formal rules are the three which have already been mentioned above.

4.3 DATA AND SELECTORS

Variables and constraints in large LP's are, generally, indexed objects. The cost vector data and the right-hand sides, therefore, must have the same indices as the variables and constraints in order to be compatible. Hence, c_j has the same indices as x_j, and r_i the same as b_i. This means for LPN, that the values in the pyramids have the same indices as the squares to which they are linked, and the same is true for triangles. Of course, some values may be zero or nonexistent. If a single pyramid has a value of zero, it is not represented. This means that the corresponding variable is not found in the objective function. Similarly, if a single triangle has a value of zero, it is not represented (a right-hand side value of zero is not written in algebraic notation). If the triangle, however, has an nonexistent value, the whole restriction is nonexistent, and therefore dropped. (The corresponding circle is not represented).

The indices of the edges representing the data in the matrix **A** vary. Since an edge is linked to a square as well as to a circle, its maximum dimension is limited to the cartesian product of their indices. An edge linked to the circle r_i and the square x_j has the indices 'i' and 'j' ($A_{i,j}$). At most, m x n individual edges are defined.

The SUM and FORALL operators of the LPL language can also be represented in the LPN formulation. They are the selectors indicated by small circles at both ends of an edge. The small circles attached to a square correspond to SUM operators and those attached to circles correspond to FORALL operators as shown in Fig. 4-7a and 4-7b.

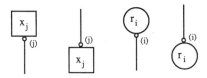

Fig. 4-7a and 4-7b.

A small circle can be labeled by indices, items or expressions of indices in order to designate over which sets summation extends. This labeling corresponds to the index notation defined in the Model Section in the LPL language. To illustrate this point, consider the following LPL notation, where 'x' is declared as 'x[i,j,k,m]'; 'i','j','k' and 'm' are sets and 'j1' is any subset of 'j':

```
r : forall[k]    sum[i,j1,m]  x[i+1,j1,k-1,] + ....
```

This notation is translated into LPN as shown in Fig. 4-8.

Note the difference in notation. If Fig. 4-8 would be translated "literally" into LPL, it would be expressed as:

```
r : forall[k-1]    sum[i+1,j1,m]  x[i,j1,k,m] + ....
```

This is not correct syntax in LPL. The expressions must be placed in 'x[.....]', in order to conform with the algebraic notation. These are, however, not fundamental differences between LPL and LPN.

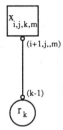

Fig. 4-8.

4.4 AGGREGATION AND DISAGGREGATION

The same LP model containing indices can be represented by different LPN structures. The LPN formulation, where all indexed objects are represented as single graphical tokens, is called the *aggregate formulation*. If, on the other hand, all indexed objects have been separated into their basic objects, in such a way that each basic object corresponds to a graphical token, then the LPN formulation is called a *disaggregate formulation*. The *partially aggregate formulation* or the *partially disaggregate formulation*, depending on one's individual point of view, is the LPN formulation where some indexed objects are aggregate or disaggregate.

The general LP, in its aggregate formulation, is shown in Fig. 4-5a. Disaggregation of this general model would depend on the indices 'i' and 'j'. Consider a concrete LP model with six columns and five rows, where i={1,..,6} and j={1,..5}. Two partially disaggregate formulations are possible as shown in Fig. 4-9a and 4-9b; the first disaggregated by the index 'i', and the second by the index 'j'.

Partially disaggregate formulations reveal some information not available in the aggregate formulation. They show, for example, that the variable x_4 is not represented in the objective function and that the restriction r_2 has a zero right-hand side.

It is taken for granted that the small circles representing selectors disappear when disaggregation takes place, since there is nothing remaining to be selected. Note also that the coefficients are not explicitly labeled. In an aggregate or partially aggregate formulation, an edge is an indexed object, since it represents many individual edges (coefficients). The coefficients of an aggregate edge may be positive, negative or even zero. This information is only revealed by disaggregating the LPN.

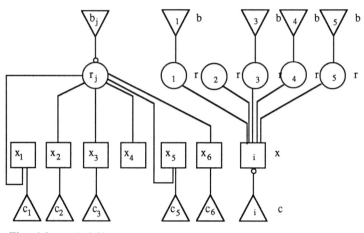

Fig. 4-9a and 4-9b.

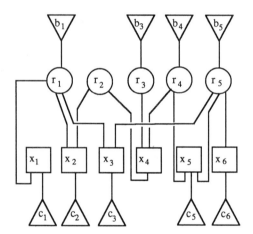

Fig. 4-9c.

The concrete, disaggregate formulation of the same model can now be deduced and expressed as shown in Fig 4-9c.

Aggregation and disaggregation are a function of the indices used in an LPN representation. The more a model is disaggregate, the more the model is revealed in detail. On the other hand, the aggregate formulation represents the most abstract and

42

basic structure of a model. Thus, a model may be analyzed on a variety of levels. These various formulations are illustrated in Fig. 4-10 by the model 'PRODUCT1.LPL' previously discussed in Chapter 3. Fig 4-10a and 4-10b represent the aggregate formulations of this model. They contain a 'loop' (an outgoing edge of y and an incoming edge, boths from the same restriction S) in variable 'y', revealing the fact that products may be also stored and are available in the the subsequent period (see also Fig. 4.14).

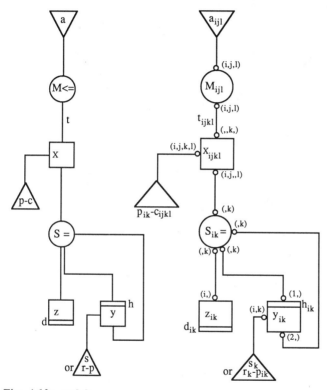

Fig. 4-10a and b.

The same model may be represented in a partially disaggregate formulation, disaggregated by the index 'i' (the periods), as shown in Fig. 4-10c.

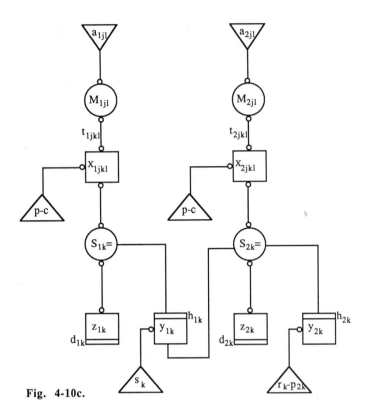

Fig. 4-10c.

Disaggregated by the different products (index k) this model would yield the
formulation shown in Fig. 4-10d.

44

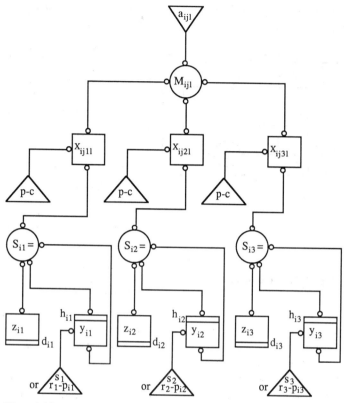

Fig. 4-10d.

4.5 GENERAL REMARKS ON LPN

LPN is a purely formal representation of the mathematical notation of an LP. The modeler is entirely free to design his model in a variety of ways. Nevertheless, it is recommended that the modeler observe some suggestions exemplified in Figs. 4-11a and 4-11b, both of which represent the same LP model.

It is evident that Fig. 4-11b reflects the structure more clearly than 4-11a. It is suggested, therefore:

- to follow a top-down design so that edges are as short as possible; squares with a top entry of edges are represented at the bottom and squares with a bottom entry of edges are represented on the top,
- to draw the edges with a minimum number of intersections between them,
- to cluster squares or circles which have the same "meaning" for the modeler.

These suggestions may contradict each other. Compromises must, therefore, be found in the lay-out of an LPN representation.

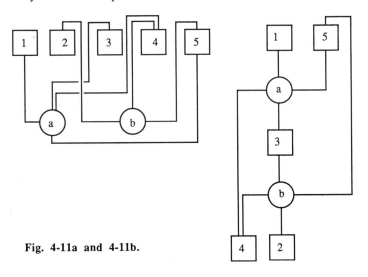

Fig. 4-11a and 4-11b.

The semantical interpretation, as well as the graphical design of an LPN representation and its elements are not formally predetermined. The modeler is free to interpret tokens, substructures or the whole LPN representation as he may require. He may, for example, in a transportation model, interpret the squares as "activities", and in a production model as "products" or "processes". Circles can have the meaning of "resources", "transformation-processes", "technological relationships", etc. Triangles may mirror "inputs", "outputs" or "capacities". Finally, the edges may reflect some "flows", which may be either "physical flows" or "information flows".

Not only single graphical tokens but also the substructures of an LPN may have a concrete significance to the modeler. A particularly useful substructure in a variety of models is the source-sink concept expressed in Fig. 4-12a and Fig. 4-12b.

Possible interpretations of these substructures are: "The sources 'x' and 'k' enter in a process 'r' and the resulting sink is 'y'"; and "the resource 'f' is distributed or partitioned into the products 'u','v' and 'w'".

Another substructure is 'reproduction' or 'recycling' as shown in Fig. 4-13 which may be interpreted as:

46

"A certain percentage 'f' of the product 'x' is re-used for its own production" (seeding or breeding in agricultural models).

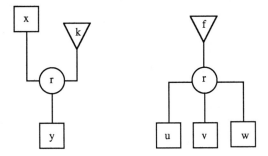

Fig. 4-12a and 4-12b.

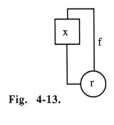

Fig. 4-13.

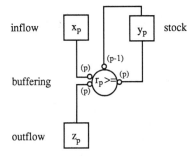

Fig. 4-14.

A third example of a substructure is 'buffering'. this is useful in production models to perform storage conditions over periods (Fig. 4-14). Consider three variables 'x' (produced quantity), 'y' (stored quantity) and 'z' (retailed quantity), all defined over a period index 'p'.

These are only some examples to show interpretative aspects of an LPN representation.

If we interpret the graphical tokens as "atoms" and substructures as "molecules", LPN, implemented as a graphics editor, might be used by a modeler, with only minimal knowledge in OR techniques, to build an entire LP model simply by putting the atoms and molecules together. Thus, LPN also gives supports in performing Step 1 in Fig. 2-1.

4.6 CAA AND LPN

The first symposium on Computer Assisted Analysis (CAA) was held at the University of Colorado, Boulder on March 24, 1980 (Greenberg 1981). CAA is a new discipline developed by Greenberg providing tools and mathematical techniques to help understand a class of models: The focus here is on LP models after they have been formulated. CAA proposes to investigate several aspects of models, such as qualitative analysis (e.g. sign solvability), embedded and hidden structures, 'what if' queries, aggregation, documentation, etc. It is not within the scope of this dissertation to repeat all the results in this research field, but it is interesting to give a brief insight into these topics. Since graph theory has been used for many of these investigations, it is perhaps enlightening to begin with these notions.

A *graph* is defined as a set of points (called *vertices*) together with a set of lines (called *edges*) joining certain pairs of distinct vertices. Two vertices (or edges) are called *adjacent* if there is an edge (or a vertex) joining them. The number of edges joining a vertex is called the *degree* of that vertex. If $E_1..E_n$ are edges, then $(E_1,E_2,...,E_n)$ is called a *path*, if E_i and E_{i-1} are adjacent for all i={2..n}. A graph is *connected*, if there is a path between any two vertices of the graph. A disconnected graph has at least two *components*. If the vertices can be partitioned into two disjoint sets so that no two vertices within the same set are adjacent, the graph is called a *bipartite graph*. A bipartite graph is said to be *complete*, if every pair of vertices in the two different sets are adjacent. It is noted as $K_{p,q}$, where p and q are the number of vertices in the two disjoint vertex sets. A graph is a *directed graph* or *digraph*, if the edges are replaced by directed edges (*arcs*). A digraph is said to be *strongly connected*, if there is an oriented path from V to V' for any two vertices V<>V'. The *strong components* within a digraph are the subgraphs of the disjoint subsets of vertices, which are strongly connected.

Any LPN representation can be transformed into a bipartite graph in the following way. Consider an entire disaggregate LPN. In this form each row and each column is drawn as a circle and a square. Each circle and square is transformed to a node and the nodes are adjacent, if a corresponding edge is found in the LPN representation. Triangles and pyramids are omitted. The newly created graph, called B, is bipartite, since there exists two disjoint vertex sets representing the rows and the columns, so that no two vertices within the same set are adjacent. A digraph, called D, with the same structure as B can be deduced from B by replacing the edges by arcs, where the direction of the arcs is determined by the sign of the corresponding coefficient with the following rule:

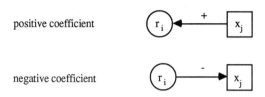

Graph B and D are identical to the "fundamental graphs" defined by Greenberg (Greenberg 1981, p.482-483). They are also bipartite consisting of two disjoint vertex sets representing rows and columns and an edge corresponding to a non-zero element in the data matrix. Greenberg introduces two other graphs which can be deduced directly from the fundamental graphs: the row graph and the column graph. The row graph consists of the nodes representing the rows in LP. Two rows are adjacent if they have a common column intersection in the matrix, or in other words, if in the fundamental graph two rows join the same column (vertex) by an edge. The column graph is defined in the same manner on columns.

These graphs are the starting point of several interesting theoretical and interpretative analyses concerning LP models. Three exemplary applications of this theory may illustrate some aspects of CAA.

Connectivity:

The two deduced graphs (row graph and column graph) are of particular interest, because they are smaller, and yet have similar properties as the fundamental graph. An important property is, for example, the following theorem:

Fundamental, column and row graphs of a corresponding model have the same number of components (Greenberg 1982, p.222). This means that if one of the three graphs is connected, then they are all connected. In this context we may mention the theorem of Bondy. The theorem is interesting because it binds the number of components of a graph without actually computing the components (see Greenberg 1981 p.487).

Structure Analysis:
Paths and cycles (closed paths), embedded in LP models, are not uncommon and pose the problem of potential infeasibility or instability. Fig. 4-15 shows the matrix form represented in graph B as a cycle.

$$
\begin{array}{ccccc}
 & j_1 & j_2 & \cdots & j_n \\
\text{OBJ} & c_1 & c_2 & \cdots & c_n \\
i_1 & -1 & & & v \\
i_2 & 1 & -1 & & \\
\cdots & & & \cdots & \\
i_n & & & & -1 \\
\end{array}
$$

Fig. 4-15. (Greenberg 1982 p.231).

The flows or the changes in activity levels amplify, dampen or remain constant depending on the value 'v' of the cycle. The significance of such considerations lies in the following expression:

if $v >= 1$ and $c_1+c_2+...+c_n < 0$, then the dual is infeasible

if $v <= 1$ and $c_1+c_2+...+c_n > 0$, then at least one activity in the cycle has a zero level. (Greenberg 1982 p.232).

Planarity:
A graph is said to be *planar*, if it can be drawn in a plane, such that no two edges meet except at a common vertex. A bipartite graph is planar, if it does not contain a subgraph K3,3 (Theorem of Kuratowski). This result is important, for example, for the graphical representation of an LPN, where the edges should not cross each other in order to preserve the overview. Topological sorting (see Knuth 1973 p.258) of the strong components in the graph gives support to a neat top-down structuring of the LPN representation. If the graph consists of one strong component, (it is strongly connected), the minimal set of edges may be searched the removal of which increases the number of strong components.

Thus, the intuitively postulated suggestions on the top-down design of an LPN representation in Section 4.5, have found their conceptual foundations in graph theory. The lay-out of an LPN representation is heavily determinate by these results and may, therefore, be automated to some degree, although not entirely, since the expression depends on the circumstances concerning how the modeler interprets his model.

4.7 CONCLUSION

LPN is a powerful tool for representing and documenting an LP model. Implemented as a graphics editor, it would also be a flexible instrument for model building, modification and analysis. Like LPL, data procurement is independent of the model building. The structure is transparent for all users concerned with the model. Thus, the LPN representation is suitable for communicating the model. The entire environment of an object, (i.e. a variable), is directly visible, and interesting for local analysis within the model. The modular expression guarantees a step by step refinement of the model.

Chapter 5

The LPL Compiler

5.1 GENERAL COMMENTS

The actual LPL compiler is a one pass compiler implemented on an IBM compatible personal computer. It has been entirely written in TURBO PASCAL using the MS-DOS operating system. Great importance has been laid on both speed and a simple user interface. The size of the models that can be handled by the compiler is limited to about 32,000 variables and constraints and 8,000 coefficients. The number of sets and items is limited by RAM, where each set and item takes about 25 bytes. The compiler reads the source LPL program from disk line per line and processes the lines directly. Declaration tables are the first to be constructed. While reading a constraint, an internal tree structure of the constraint is built and the constraint is written directly on the disk. Therefore, any preceding constraints are 'forgotten' by the compiler but not the preceding declarations. The same declaration may, thus, be used in different submodels. The compiler first produces a PASCAL direct access file which is sorted by restrictions with the filename extension '.RES'. Then this file is re-read after the compilation and a second file with the filename extension '.VAR' is produced, and sorted by variables. These two files contain redundant information in order to produce other representations of the model, (i.e. an MPSX standard file).

5.2 THE SCHEME

Before the LPL package can be used, LPL programs need to be created. This can be done by the integrated text editor or any other (non-document) text editor like WordStar. The filename of an LPL program must contain the extension '.LPL'. Appendix 2 illustrates additional samples of LPL programs. It is not necessary to store the LPL programs on the same disk as the LPL compiler.

An LPL program is a complete and readable formulation of an LP problem, and it can also be used for documentation, independent of any optimization software. The LPL compiler produces two internal files, a restrictions sorted file and a variables sorted file. These two files can be used to create the coded form for different optimization software packages or various readable output files, such as an equation listing or a matrix picture (see Fig. 5-1). The modules which produce these different output files are also available with the LPL compiler.

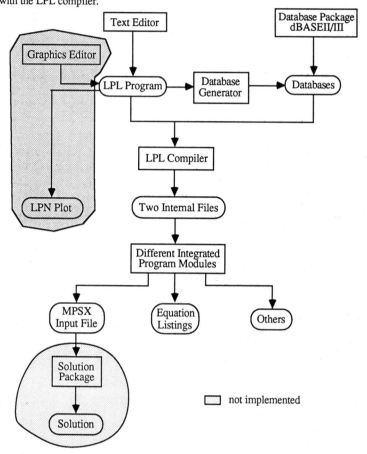

Fig. 5-1.

The LPN Plot and solution procedures illustrated in the above scheme are not actually implemented in the present LPL environment, but they are mentioned in Fig. 5-1 in order to give the reader an overview of these possibilities.

5.3 THE MAIN MENU

After the editing an LPL program by a text editor, the command

may be entered. This command takes the user to the Main menu.
The screen clears and displays the following menu, this time with the command letters
highlighted.

```
Working Model:                       Version 2.11

  Main:    Compile           Edit            eXit

  Files:   eQuationListing(.EQU)   Picture(.PIC)    NameListing(.NAM)

  Options: print Intern file    create MPSX file  create empty dBase

  Solution:  Run solution        printSolution


  Enter an Option:
```

This menu shows the commands available while working with LPL. A command is
activated by pressing the associated letter. No subsequent <RETURN> is needed. The
command is executed immediately, and any illegal entry will be ignored.
The following sections describe each command in detail. The output produced by these
commands are explained by the example 'ROBOT1.LPL' already used in Chapter 3.

Working Model Selection:
The command **W** selects a working model, (e.g. the new active model). This command
will bring up the line:

Enter Modelname:

The user must then respond with any legal filename (preceded by a drive specification),
not containing an extension. The user may enter, for example, 'ROBOT1' and terminate
this filename with a <RETURN>.

Compile Selection:
The command **C** compiles the working model written in LPL. The LPL program is read
from disk and the compiler produces two additional files with the same name as the
working model name and the extensions '.RES' and '.VAR', ('ROBOT1.RES' and
'ROBOT1.VAR'). Since these files are PASCAL direct access files, they cannot be

55

listed directly. They may, however, be listed after compiling with the command I, explained below. The compilation may take a few minutes depending on the length of the LPL program. An editor is included within the LPL package. Hence, a compiling error within an LPL program will stop the compilation and allow the modeler to automatically activate the editor in order to correct the error.

Edit Selection:

The command **E** leads the user into a WordStar-like editor.

(See Hürlimann T., Reference Manual for the LPL Modeling Language for the editor commands).

Exit Selection:

The command **X** is used to leave the LPL system.

Equation Listing Selection:

The command **Q** prints all the equations of the active model either on the screen or into a file with the extension, '.EQU'. Hence, the file 'ROBOT1.EQU' would look like:

```
PRO0:  + 5.00*MARIE + 5.00*JULES <=  350.000
PRO1:  + 4.00*MARIE + 8.00*JULES <=  480.000
PRO2:  + 6.00*MARIE + 2.00*JULES <=  300.000
ORD3:  + MARIE >=   20.000
ORD4:  + JULES >=   15.000
MAX5:  + 300.00*MARIE + 200.00*JULES MA    0.000
```

The objective function has an operator 'MA' or 'MI' depending on whether the function is meant to maximize or minimize. The line width may be controlled in order to have a conform (paper) format.

Picture Selection:

The command **P** prints the coefficient matrix either on the screen or into a file with the extension, '.PIC'. The variables are listed in columns and the restrictions in rows. The non-zero elements are printed as 'x' and the zero elements as '.', (a dot). If the matrix is larger than the screen or paper width of the printer, it will be printed as subblocks from left to right and from top to bottom.

The file 'ROBOT1.PIC' has the following format:

```
                MJ
                AU
                RL
                IE
                ES

     PRO0       xx
     PRO1       xx
     PRO2       xx
     ORD3       x.
     ORD4       .x
     MAX5       xx
```

Nomenclature Listing Selection:

The command **N** prints a listing of all the declared items either on the screen or into a file with the extension, '.NOM'. Sets are listed with their elements, single coefficient names with their values and variable names in their internal and external notations. The command N creates the file 'ROBOT1.NOM', which looks like:

```
STRUCTURE OF THE MODEL:
^^^^^^^^^^^^^^^^^^^^^^^^

SETS:
ROBOTS (2) :MARIE JULES
PRODUCTIONSTEPS (3) :PRODUCTION MOUNTING TESTING

COEFFICIENTS:
PRICE (ROBOTS ) (2)
    PRICE (MARIE) = 300.00
    PRICE (JULES) = 200.00
ORDERED (ROBOTS ) (2)
    ORDERED (MARIE) =  20.00
    ORDERED (JULES) =  15.00
CAPACITY (PRODUCTIONSTEPS ) (3)
    CAPACITY (PRODUCTION) = 350.00
    CAPACITY (MOUNTING) = 480.00
    CAPACITY (TESTING) = 300.00
TIMECOSTS (ROBOTS PRODUCTIONSTEPS ) (6)
    TIMECOSTS (MARIE,PRODUCTION) =   5.00
    TIMECOSTS (MARIE,MOUNTING) =   4.00
    TIMECOSTS (MARIE,TESTING) =   6.00
    TIMECOSTS (JULES,PRODUCTION) =   5.00
    TIMECOSTS (JULES,MOUNTING) =   8.00
    TIMECOSTS (JULES,TESTING) =   2.00

VARIABLES:
NUMBER (ROBOTS ) (2)
    MARIE   = NUMBER (MARIE)
    JULES   = NUMBER (JULES)
```

This file is of special interest, if sets and indexed coefficients, as well as indexed variables have been defined. First the sets, and then the individual coefficients and variables with there internal and external notations, are listed.

Print Internal File Selection:
The command **I** writes the generated files (with extensions '.RES' or '.VAR') in a readable form either on the screen or in two files with extensions, 'REI' and 'VAI':

The file 'ROBOT1.RAI':

```
R   0     PROO      0.00
V   1     MARIE     5.00
V   2     JULES     5.00
O   0      <=     350.00
  R   1     PRO1      0.00
V   1     MARIE     4.00
V   2     JULES     8.00
O   0      <=     480.00
  R   2     PRO2      0.00
V   1     MARIE     6.00
V   2     JULES     2.00
O   0      <=     300.00
  R   3     ORD3      0.00
V   1     MARIE     1.00
O   0      >=      20.00
  R   4     ORD4      0.00
V   2     JULES     1.00
O   0      >=      15.00
  R   5     MAX5      0.00
V   1     MARIE   300.00
V   2     JULES   200.00
O   0      MA       0.00
```

The file 'ROBOT1.VAI':

```
V   1     MARIE     0.00
  R   0     PROO      5.00
  R   1     PRO1      4.00
  R   2     PRO2      6.00
  R   3     ORD3      1.00
  R   5     MAX5    300.00
V   2     JULES     0.00
  R   0     PROO      5.00
  R   1     PRO1      8.00
  R   2     PRO2      2.00
  R   4     ORD4      1.00
  R   5     MAX5    200.00
```

The first file is ordered by restrictions and the second by variables. Each file consists of a number of lines with four entries per line.

The first entry is the letter 'R', 'V' or 'O', depending on the line type, (i.e. a Restriction

58

name, a Variable name or a right-hand side with the Operator). The second entry is a unique number corresponding to an individual variable restriction. This number is used by the LPL package to identify the variable or restriction. It is also used by the default compiler directive to produce a unique internal column and row name. The third entry is either the internal restriction name, the variable name or the operator created by the compiler. They are used in the MPSX file. The fourth element indicates the corresponding real coefficient or the right-hand side of an equation.

Create MPSX File Selection:
The command **M** is used to create the whole MPSX standard input file. The filename has the extension, '.MPS'. This file may use a large amount of disk space.
The command M in our example, creates the MPSX standard input file 'ROBOT1.MPS', which is shown below:

```
NAME            ROBOT1
ROWS
  L   PRO0
  L   PRO1
  L   PRO2
  N   MAX5
COLUMNS
      MARIE     PRO0      5
      MARIE     PRO1      4
      MARIE     PRO2      6
      MARIE     MAX5      300
      JULES     PRO0      5
      JULES     PRO1      8
      JULES     PRO2      2
      JULES     MAX5      200
RHS
      ..RHS     PRO0      350
      ..RHS     PRO1      480
      ..RHS     PRO2      300
BOUNDS
  LO BOUNDS     MARIE     20
  LO BOUNDS     JULES     15
ENDATA
```

The file 'ROBOT1.MPS' is a simple text file (ASCII file). It may be printed using the command TYPE in MS-DOS and then transferred to a host machine where the model may be solved.

Create Empty dBASE Selection:
The command **D** creates empty dBASEII files from a maketable option in the LPL program. All data are set to the nonexistent value (-99.99).

Other Options Selection:

The command **O** displays another menu on the screen. From this menu the user may select other less important options such as reading an MPSX file in order to produce the two internal files with extension names, '.RES' and '.VAR'.

Run Solution Selection:

The command **R** prepares a batch file named 'S.BAT'. This file is used by the LP83 package (Sunset 1985) to calculate the solution for small LP problems. LPL is automatically exited in order to execute the batch file. After terminating the solution procedures, the batch automatically returns to the LPL mainmenu.

Print Solution Selection:

Finally, the command **S** prints the solution file (with the extension '.PRN'), produced by the LP83 package, on the screen. It is obvious that the commands **R** and **S** can be used only for small and medium size LP models (limited by the package LP83). Larger models need to be transferred to a host machine to be solved.

5.4 ADDITIONAL REMARKS ON THE IMPLEMENTATION

Since LPL accepts only linear constraints, (even expressions like 'x/x' are not allowed), it is evident that non-linear expressions are detected by the compiler and an error message is produced.

If the following conditions are met, parts or even entire constraints are dropped:

- terms are omitted, if the corresponding coefficient is zero or nonexistent, or if the variable is nonexistent.

- constraints are omitted, if the right-hand side is nonexistent, or if one term is left in the restriction.

Several objective functions are allowed in the same LPL program. The compiler produces the operator 'MA' for a maximizing, and 'MI' for a minimizing function.

5.5 BENCH MARKS

All of the LPL examples mentioned in this dissertation are compiled in a few seconds except for the 'EP.LPL' model. The MPSX file is produced instantly. Thus, the LPL package may also be useful for solving small LP problems in a teaching environment.

The entire EP model consisting of 1,471 constraints, 1,769 variables and 6,713 non-zero elements in the matrix, takes five minutes to be compiled on an IBM AT compatible computer (with a 20 MB harddisk and a 640 kB RAM) and an additional 2,5 minutes to produce the whole MPSX standard file. This file uses 243,104 bytes on disk. It may be directly transferred to the IBM MPS standard package for solution purposes, with no necessary modifications. Any recompilation of the model erases the internal files of the preceding run and produces new files.

LPL is certainly a powerful language because of its complex index mechanism. There are, however, a few more delicate points which should be mentioned. Small changes made to some indices or items may have an important influence on the model structure. The item identifiers have been found to be particularly ticklish. The compiler compares the items in the different sets, and if they have the same spelling, they are recognized to be identical.

5.6 ERROR MESSAGES

The following is a listing of error messages from the LPL compiler. When the compiler encounters a syntax error, it will print the error number with a message. The number corresponds to the number listed below. After each error the compiler stops and the editor is started in order to allow the user to correct the error.

```
500  ; expected
501  MODEL expected
502  Identifier expected (or reserved word used)
503  File not found
504  Operator expected
505  ) expected
506  Number expected
507  = expected
508  Apostrophe expected
509  ( , MAKETABLE , FILETABLE expected
510  SetIdentifier or ( expected
511  SetIdentifier expected
512  END expected
513  SetIdentifier or Element expected
514  Unknown item
515  Too many fields in dBASEII structure
516  Unknown identifier
517  This identifier is not allowed here
518  This is not a linear equation
519  Corresponding # <setidentifier> not found in the same equation
520  Incorrect identifier
521  This file is not a dBASEII/III datafile
522  Only numerical and alphanumerical fields are allowed in the file
523  Invalid or empty dBASEII/III file
524  Field name is not of type 'character'
525  CoefficientIdentifier expected
526  Duplicated Set Declaration
527  Incorrect Set range
528  Duplicated Element Declaration
529  Element identifier expected
```

530 Duplicated declaration
531 Incorrect path or element not found
532 0..4 expected
533 Illegal number of set identifier in the index list
535 No matching length of file
536 No matching width of records in file
537] expected
538 No corresponding set identifier in sum index list

APPENDICES

The syntax of LPL is presented here using the formalism known as the extended extended Backus-Naur Form used by N. Wirth. The following symbols are metasymbols, unless they are included in apostrophes, (e.g. '{' or '['):

::= means "is defined as" (defines a production)
| means "or"
{ } enclose items which may be repeated zero or more times
[ ] enclose items which may be repeated zero or one time

All other symbols are part of LPL. Reserved words are printed entirely in uppercase letters. The beginning symbol is 'Program'. Lower and uppercase letters within the syntax are treated identically.

```
AliasName ::= AnyString
AnyString ::= Char { Char }
Block ::= DeclarationSection ModelSection
Char ::= Digit | Letter | Special
Coefficient ::= CoefficientIdentifier = [(| Data [)]
              | IndexedCoefficient = ( Data { [,] Data } )
              | IndexedCoefficient = FILETABLE QuotedString
              | IndexedCoefficient = MAKETABLE QuotedString [ number ]
CoefficientDeclaration ::= COEF Coefficient { [;] Coefficient } [;]
CoefficientIdentifier ::= Identifier
Comment ::= '{' AnyString '}'
          | (* AnyString *)
Data ::= Number | -
DeclarationSection ::= [SetDeclaration]
                       [CoefficientDeclaration]
                       VariableDeclaration
                       [ResDeclaration]
Digit ::= 1 | 2 | 3 | 4 | 5 | 6 | 7 | 8 | 9 | 0
Element ::= ElementIdentifier [: ElementIdentifier] [' AliasName '] {/
Number}
          | SetIdentifier [=] ElementList
ElementIdentifier ::= Identifier | Number
ElementList ::= ( Element { [,] Element } )
EquationExpression ::= [Sign] EquationTerm { Sign EquationTerm }
EquationTerm ::= [SumOverTerm] SimpleEquationTerm
EquFactor ::= VariableIdenifier [ExpressionIndexList]
            | CoefficientIdentifier [ExpressionIndexList]
            | UnsignedNumber
            | ( EquationExpression )
            | MIN [( ObjectFunctionIdentifier )]
            | MAX [( ObjectFunctionIdentifier )]
ExpressionIndexList ::= LeftPar SetExpression { , SetExpression } RightPar
ForallTerm ::= FORALL SumIndexList
Identifier ::= Letter { LetterOrDigit }
```

63

```
IndexedCoefficient ::= CoefficientIdentifier IdentifierList
IndexList ::= SimpleIndexList | SumIndexList | ExpressionIndexList
LeftPar ::= ( | '['
Letter ::= A | B | .... | Y | Z | _ | a | b | .... | y | z
LetterOrDigit ::= Letter | Digit
LinearEquation ::= MultipleLinearEquation | SimpleLinearEquation
ModelSection ::= MODEL Statement { ; Statement }
MultipleLinearEquation ::= [RestrictionName :]
                           [ForallTerm] SimpleLinearEquation
MultiplingSign ::= * | /
Number ::= [Sign] UnsignedNumber
ObjectFunctionIdentifier ::= Identifier
Operator ::= <> | = | <= | >= | < | >
Program ::= [ ProgramHeading ] Block { Block } END
ProgramHeading ::= PROGRAM ProgramIdentifier ;
QuotedString ::= ' AnyString '
ResDeclaration ::= RES Variable { [;] Variable } [;]
RestrictionName ::= Identifier | QuotedString
RightPar ::= ) | ']'
Set ::= SetIdentifier {/ CoefficientIdentifier } [=] ElementList
        | SetIdentifier [=] FILETABLE QuotedString Number [Number]
SetDeclaration ::= SET { Set [;] }
SetExpression ::= [Sign] SetTerm { Sign SetTerm }
SetFactor ::= SetIdentifierPath
SetIdentifier ::= Identifier
SetIdentifierPath ::= [:]{ SetIdentifier : } SetOrElementIdentifier
SetOrElementIdentifier ::= SetIdentifier | ElementIdentifier
SetTerm ::= SetFactor { MultliplingSign SetFactor }
Sign ::= + | -
SimpleEquationTerm ::= EquFactor { MultiplyingSign EquFactor }
SimpleIndexList ::= LeftPar SetIdentifierPath { , SetIdentifierPath }
RightPar
SimpleLinearEquation ::= EquationExpression Operator EquationExpression
Special ::= + | - | * | / | = | < | > | ( | ) | '[' | ']' | '{' | '}' | .
            | , | : | ; | ' | # | &
Statement ::= [ LinearEquation ]
SumIndexElement ::= [Symbol] SetIdentifier
SumIndexList ::= LeftPar SumIndexElement { , SumIndexElement } RightPar
SumOverTerm ::= SUM SumIndexList
Symbol ::= # | & | #& | &# | *
UnsignedInteger ::= Digit { Digit }
UnsignedNumber ::= UnsignedInteger [. UnsignedInteger]
Variable ::= VariableIdentifier [SimpleIndexList]
             | VariableIdentifier LIKE CoefficientIdentifier
VariableDeclaration ::= VAR Variable { [;] Variable } [;]
VarIdentifier ::= Identifier
```

The reserved words are:

```
COEF  END  FILETABLE  FORALL  LIKE  MAKETABLE
MAX  MIN  MODEL  PROGRAM  RES  SET  SUM  VAR
```

64

Several LPL programming examples have been used in this dissertation. Additional examples are listed below in order to show the different aspects of the LPL language. Example 1 is exactly the same model as 'PRODUCT1.LPL' seen earlier in Chapter 3 but with more explicit identifiers.

EXAMPLE 1   PRODUCT.LPL:

```
(* PRODUCT.LPL: see model 'PRODUCT1.LPL'
(*************************************)
{$C'T'+a1+i2(1,2)+i3(1,2)+i4(1,2)+v(1,2)   this is a compiler directive}

Set
    Periods = (Summer'1' Winter'2')
    ProductionMode = (normal  overtime)
    {three products (P1,P2,P3) with their storing costs, storing capacity
    and resalevalue per unit}
    Products /Store/StoreCapa/ResaleValue =
            (P1/1/20/2   P2/1/20/2   P3/1/-/1);
    Machines = (M1:M3)

Coef
    MachineTable(Periods,ProductionMode,Products,Machines) =
                (4 7 3   5 6 -   6 6 -
                 3 6 2   4 5 -   5 5 -
                 5 8 4   6 7 -   7 7 -
                 4 7 3   5 6 -   5 6 -)
    cost(Periods,ProductionMode,Products,Machines) =
                (2 4 1   3 3 -   4 2 -
                 3 5 2   4 4 -   5 3 -
                 3 5 2   4 4 -   5 3 -
                 4 6 3   5 5 -   6 4 -)
    MachAvail(Periods,ProductionMode,Machines) =
                (100 100 40   80  90 30
                 110 110 50   90 100 40)
    Price(Periods,Products)  = (10 10  9   11 11 10)
    Demands(Periods,Products) = (25 30 30   30 25 25)

Var
    QUANTITY like MachineTable
    STORED(Periods,Products)
    SOLD(Periods,Products)
Res
    Mach_Avail(Periods,ProductionMode,Machines)
    Stock1(Products); Stock2(Products)
    Demand(Periods,Products); Bound(Products)

Model
    (* the profit function: *)
    sum[Periods,ProductionMode,Products,Machines](Price-Cost)*QUANTITY
    - sum[Products]Store*STORED[Summer,]
    + sum[Products](ResaleValue-Price[Winter,])*STORED[Winter,]
    = MAX(profit);
```

65

```
(* constraints of machine availability: *)
MACH_AVAIL: sum[products] MachineTable * QUANTITY  <=  MachAvail;
(* stock balances in the two periods *)
STOCK1: sum[ProductionMode,machines] QUANTITY[summer,,,]
        = STORED[summer,] + SOLD[summer,] ;
STOCK2: sum[ProductionMode,machines] QUANTITY[winter,,,] + STORED[summer,]
        = STORED[winter,] + SOLD[winter,] ;
(* minimum demands to be satisfied *)
DEMAND: SOLD >= demands;
(* upper bound on storage *)
BOUND : STORED[summer,]  <=  StoreCapa;
End
```

The next example was mentioned in Chapter 2 and was formulated by Katz (1980) in the LPMODEL language. Below is the LPL formulation:

Example 2   CROP.LPL:

```
(* CROP.LPL: Example used by Katz S. (IBM Systems Journal 19:4,1980,
   p.505-520, Appendix B) written in the modeling language LPMODEL. *)
(******************************************************)
Program Crop_Production;
set
  Month/Water_BND = (May/200000   June/260000   July/270000)
  Crop/Labor/Profit/Ceiling =  (Cotton/2.9/6453/2000  Onion/2.7/6110/250
                    Pear/1/4814/500 Avocado/1.5/8813/800)
  Field = (Cotton Onion)
coef
  Land = 2700     Field_Land = 1850     Labor_Tot = 5850
  Water(Crop,Month) = ( 65 80 90 , - 60 - , - 53 64 , - 75 85 )
var  CropVar(Crop)

model
  sum(Crop) CropVar <= Land;
  sum(Field) CropVar <= Field_Land;
  forall(month) sum(Crop) Water*CropVar <= Water_BND;
  sum(Crop)  Labor*CropVar <= Labor_Tot;
  forall(Crop)  CropVar <= Ceiling;
  sum(Crop)  Profit*CropVar = Max
end
```

Example 3 was formulated by SCICON (1984) to illustrate the MGG modeling language. Below is the LPL program formulation for the same model:

Example 3   TRAVEL.LPL

```
(* TRAVEL.LPL: Example used by SCICON Ltd. (OR Spectrum, 1984, 6:125-130)
   to illustrate the MGG modeling language. (below in LPL).
(**********************************************************************)
```

66

```
{$Cv(1,5)+i1(1,2)+i2(1,2)+i3(1,2)    compiler directive}
set
   f/Time1/Maxtr1/Cost1 = (Air/0.8/10/300  Bus/6/15/100  Train/10/100/ 60)
   s/Time2/Maxtr2/Cost2 = (Air/2.1/20/800  Bus/12/8/200  Train/24/100/160)
   g/Numgrd/Valtim = (Manager/12/20  Stuff/18/15)
coef
   Wait(f,s) = ( 7.1  1.5  2 , 0.9  5  1 , 1.3  0.6  1.5 )
   fareMx = 20000
var
   x(g,f,s)   hours(g)   tfare

model
   sum(g)  Valtim*hours + tfare = MIN;
   forall(g)  sum(f,s)  X = Numgrd;
   forall(f)  sum(g,s)  X <= Maxtr1;
   forall(s)  sum(g,f)  X <= Maxtr2;
   sum(g,f,s)  (Cost1+Cost2)*X = tfare;
   forall(g)  sum(f,s)  (Time1+Wait+Time2)*X = hours;
   tfare  <= fareMx;
   forall(s)  X(Manager,Train,) = 0;  {ensures that manager do}
   forall(f)  X(Manager,,Train) = 0  {not take the train}
end
```

Examples 4 and 5 represent the same network problem. Example 5 is a more general formulation.

Example 4:

```
(* NETWORK.IPL: a simple network problem:
   Problem: Find the maximum flow in the following network

                   b . . . . . 8 e
            12 .           10   .
             .   .            . 9   .
             .     .        .     .     .
           .         .    .         .     .
          .            . .            .     .
         .             9 .              .    30
        a . . . . .10 c                   .     g
         .             9 .                .    30
          .             .   .           .     .
           .            .     .       .     .
             .          .       .   .     .
               .        . .       . .   .
                14 .              8 8 .
                   d . . . . . 7 f

Reference: [Sunset Software,1985,p.11-1]
(***************************************************)

{$Ci1(1,2)  compiler directive}

set
   flows/bounds = (ab/12,ac/10,ad/14,bc/9,be/10,ce/10,
                   cf/8,dc/9,df/7,ef/8,eg/30,fe/9,fg/30);
```

67

```
var
  X(flows);

model
  { constraints on flows between nodes }
  B :  X(ab) - X(bc) - X(be) = 0;
  C :  X(ac) + X(bc) + X(dc) - X(ce) - X(cf) = 0;
  D :  X(ad) - X(dc) - X(df) = 0;
  E :  X(be) + X(ce) + X(fe) - X(ef) - X(eg) = 0;
  F :  X(cf) + X(df) + X(ef) - X(fe) - X(fg) = 0;
  { bounds }
    forall(flows) X(flows) <= bounds;
  { objective function }
    X(eg) + X(fg) = max(flow)
end
```

Example 5:

```
(* NETWORK1.IPL: This is exactly the same model as 'NETWORK.IPL'
   but with another - a more general - IPL formulation
(************************************************************)

{$Ci1(1,2)+'.'+i2(1,2)  compiler directive}

SET
  { definition of the node set }
  nodes = (source rely(b,c,d,e,f) sink);
  nodes1 = (source rely(b,c,d,e,f) sink);

COEF
  flows[nodes,nodes1] =    { the flows matrix }
                  { to source rely  b   c   d   e   f  sink}
           {---------------------------------------------------}
           {from source} (  -    -  12  10  14   -   -   -
                 {rely }    -    -   -   -   -   -   -   -
                 {b    }    -    -   -   9   -  10   -   -
                 {c    }    -    -   -   -   -  10   8   -
                 {d    }    -    -   -   9   -   -   7   -
                 {e    }    -    -   -   -   -   -   8  30
                 {f    }    -    -   -   -   -   9   -  30
                 {sink }    -    -   -   -   -   -   -   - );

VAR
  x like flows

MODEL
  { bounds on the single flows }
    forall[&nodes,&nodes1] x <= flows ;
  { constraints }
    forall[rely] sum[&nodes] x[,rely] = sum[&nodes1] x[rely,];
  { objective function }
    sum[rely] x[,sink] = max(flow);
END
```

Example 6: compares PAM formulation with LPL formulation:

```
(* TRANS.LPL: LPL Formulation of the transport example in
   'PAM Overview' written by J. B. Creegan, jr.
   *************************************************************
   First let us write down the model in PAM matrix description form:

           DATA    Z:MATRIX
   **       MAKE     SHIP     RTYPE     RHS
   COST    PRCOST   TRCOST    <>
   CAPACITY /1                <        PRCAP
   BALANCE  /-1      /1       =        0
   DEMAND            /1       >        ORDERS

           DATA    Z:COLUMNS
   **       MAKE     SHIP
   LIT      PR       SH
   PRODUCT PRODUCT   PRODUCT
   SOURCE   PLANT    PLANT
   DEST              CUSTOMER
   *

           DATA    Z:ROWS
   **       LIT    PRODUCT   SOURCE   DEST
   CAPACITY CAP              PLANT
   BALANCE  BAL    PRODUCT   PLANT
   DEMAND   DEM    PRODUCT            CUSTOMER

           DATA    Z:DATA
   **       TABLE      STUB      HEAD
   TRCOST   TRCOST     SOURCE    DEST
   PRCOST   PRCOST     PRODUCT   SOURCE
   PRCAP    CAPACITY   SOURCE    TONS
   ORDERS   DEMAND     DEST      TONS
   *
           DATA    T:TRCOST
   **     BA     PH     WA     RI
   SS    3.52   9.47   0.38   8.63
   HD    2.04   6.61   7.22   9.97

           DATA    T:PRCOST
   **    { here follow the data }

           DATA    T:PRCAP
   **    { here follow the data }

           DATA    T:ORDERS
   **    { here follow the data }


   ********************** end PAM description ***********************
```

```
************************The IPL formulation now: ******************)
  {$Cv(1,2)+i1(1,2)+i2(1,2)+i3(1,2)   column names}
  {$Rv(1,3)+i1(1,2)+i2(1,2)           row names}


SET   {——called 'attributes' in PAM——}
  source =      ( SS  HD )
  destination = ( BA  PH  WA  RI )
  product   =   ( P1  P2 P3 )   {not specified in the example}


COEF  {——called 'data' in PAM——}
  trcost[source,destination] = { BA    PH    WA    RI }
                             ( 3.52  9.47  0.38  8.63   {SS}
                               2.04  6.61  7.22  9.97 ) {HD}
  {all following data are not explicitly in the example: }
  prcost[source,product] =   ( 4.22  5.05  4.60
                               1.45  2.45  2.03 )
  prCap[source]       = ( 500   600 )
  orders[destination] = ( 120   100   30  234 )


VAR   {——called 'classes of activities' in PAM——}
  PR[product,source]              {MAKE}
  SH[product,source,destination]  {SHIP}


RES   {——called 'classes of constraints' in PAM——}
  Capacity[source]
  Balance[product,source]
  Demand[product,destination]


MODEL {——replaces the central matrix descriptive table in PAM——}
  Costs  :  SUM[product,source]
                (prcost*PR+SUM[destination] trcost*SH) = MIN;
  Capacity: SUM[product]  PR < prCap;
  Balance : PR = SUM[destination] SH;
  Demand  : SUM[source]  SH > orders
END
```

The EP model, mentioned several times in this dissertation, is a multiperiodic model containing six periods (P1-P6) equivalent to six planning years. Each period contains four sectors and are called the plant, animal, nourishment and storage sector (Pflanzen-, Tier-, Ernährungs- und Lagersektor). The major decision variables for each period are crop areas (PC), animal population (PL), emergency stocks (Y) and the average nourishment ratio per capita (R). The model contains two objective, which are optimized during two calculation steps. The first objective maximizes the calories of an average nourishment ratio in period P5. which is the period containing the most arable land and the lowest animal population. The second objective is the storage cost which is minimized.

The following listing is the entire LPL program of this model. Most data are stored on dBASEIII tables.

```
PROGRAM Ernaehrungs_Plan_von_Dr_Egli;
(***********************************)

{$Vi1(3,1)+'.'+v(1,2)+a3+a2   Interne Variablennamen }

(********************* Pflanzen Sektor *********************)
{ Flaechenbeziehungen }
{ ------------------- }
SET Flaechen/FlaechenVorgaben    {in 10'000 ha}

    (Berg'MTT'
      (Alpweiden'M20' Nutzflaeche'MTL'
        (Naturwiesen'M19' Fruchtfolge'MTB'
          (Kunstwiesen'M18'/0.675 Acker'MTA'
            (Brotgetreide'M03' (Winterweizen'M00'/0.22
                                Sommerweizen'M01'/0.083
                                Roggen'M02'/0.042 Triticale'M25'/0)
             Futtergetreide'M08' (Sommergerste'M05'/0.704
                                  Hafer'M06'/0.22)
             Hackfruechte'M12'   (Kartoffel'M09'/0.25
                                  Gemuese'M15'/0.02)
      ) ) ) )
    Tal'TT'
      (Zwischenfrucht'17' Nutzflaeche'TL'
        (Naturwiesen'19' Fruchtfolge'TB'
          (Kunstwiesen'18'/10 Acker'TA'
            (Brotgetreide'03'    (Winterweizen'00'/8.625
                                  Sommerweizen'01'/0.77
                                  Roggen'02'/0.34 Triticale'25'/0.08)
             Futtergetreide'08'  (Wintergerste'04'/3.643
                                  Sommergerste'05'/1.477
                                  Hafer'06'/0.987
                                  KoernerMais'07'/1.913
                                  SaatKoernerMais'S07'/0.037
                                  GruenHafer'S08'/0.056)
             Hackfruechte'12'  (Kartoffel'09'/1.76
```

71

```
                              Zuckerrueben'10'/1.425
                              Futterrueben'11'/0.258
                              Raps'13'/1.501 Bohnen'14'/0.022
                              EiweissErbsen'26'/0.046
                              Gemuese'15'/1.068 SiloMais'16'/4.47
                              PflanzKartoffeln '29'/0.2)
            ) ) ) )
    );
  Perioden(PE0:PE6); P(PE0:PE5); P1(PE1:PE5); P2(PE1:PE4);
  P3(PE2:PE5); P4(PE1:PE3); P5(PE1:PE6)
  P6(PE0:PE4)    {Perioden}  P8(PE3:PE5);

COEF   a[P3] = ( 0.27  0.26  0.25  0.25 )
       b[P3] = ( 0.27  0.21  0.18  0.18 )

VAR   PC(P,Flaechen);              { Flaechen in 10'000 ha }

MODEL
  { Flaechenaufteilungen }
  PD: forall[P1,#Flaechen] PC = sum[*Flaechen] PC;
  { Fruchtfolgebeziehungen im Berg }
  MMGRFE: forall[P3] 0.29*PC[P3,:Berg:FruchtFolge]
          <= PC[P3,:Berg:BrotGetreide] + PC[P3,:Berg:FutterGetreide];
  MMROOT: forall[P3] 0.13*PC[P3,:Berg:FruchtFolge]
          <= PC[P3,:Berg:HackFruechte] ;
  MXSGRS: forall[P3] b * PC[P3,:Berg:FruchtFolge]
          >= PC[P3,:Berg:KunstWiesen] ;
  MZCRR1: forall[P3] 0.3*PC[P3,:Berg:BrotGetreide]
          <= PC[P3,:Berg:Roggen] ;
  MZCRR2: forall[P3] 0.8*PC[P3,:Berg:BrotGetreide] +
          0.8*PC[P3,:Berg:FutterGetreide] >=
          + PC[P3,:Berg:WinterWeizen] + PC[P3,:Berg:SommerWeizen] +
          PC[P3,:Berg:SommerGerste] ;
  MZCRR5: forall[P3] 0.3*PC[P3,:Berg:FutterGetreide] >=
          PC[P3,:Berg:Hafer] ;
  MZCRR7: forall[P3] 0.5*PC[P3,:Berg:WinterWeizen] >=
          PC[P3,:Berg:SommerWeizen] ;
  { Fruchtfolgebeziehungen im Tal }
  PMGRFE: forall[P3] 0.29*PC[P3,:Tal:FruchtFolge]
          <= PC[P3,:Tal:BrotGetreide] + PC[P3,:Tal:FutterGetreide] ;
  PMROOT: forall[P3] 0.13*PC[P3,:Tal:FruchtFolge] <=
          PC[P3,:Tal:HackFruechte] ;
  PMSGRS: forall[P3] 0.2*PC[P3,:Tal:FruchtFolge] <=
          PC[P3,:Tal:KunstWiesen] ;
  PXGRFE: forall[P3] 0.6*PC[P3,:Tal:FruchtFolge]
          >= PC[P3,:Tal:BrotGetreide] + PC[P3,:Tal:FutterGetreide] ;
  PXROOT: forall[P3] 0.45*PC[P3,:Tal:FruchtFolge] >=
          PC[P3,:Tal:HackFruechte] ;
  PXSGRS: forall[P3] a * PC[P3,:Tal:FruchtFolge] >=
          PC[P3,:Tal:KunstWiesen] ;
  PZCRR1: forall[P3] 0.15*PC[P3,:Tal:WinterWeizen] +
          0.15*PC[P3,:Tal:SommerWeizen] >=
          PC[P3,:Tal:Roggen] ;
  PZCRR2: forall[P3] 0.8*PC[P3,:Tal:BrotGetreide] +
          0.8*PC[P3,:Tal:FutterGetreide] >=
          PC[P3,:Tal:WinterWeizen]
          + PC[P3,:Tal:SommerWeizen] + PC[P3,:Tal:SommerGerste] +
          PC[P3,:Tal:WinterGerste] ;
```

```
PZCRR4: forall[P3] 0.3*PC[P3,:Tal:WinterGerste] <=
        0.7*PC[P3,:Tal:SommerGerste] ;
PZCRR5: forall[P3] 0.5*PC[P3,:Tal:FutterGetreide]   >=
        PC[P3,:Tal:Hafer] ;
PZCRR6: forall[P1] 0.5*PC[P1,:Tal:WinterWeizen] +
        0.5*PC[P1,:Tal:WinterGerste]
        + 0.5*PC[P1,:Tal:Hafer] + 0.5*PC[P1,:Tal:Raps] >=
        PC[P1,:Tal:ZwischenFrucht] ;
PZCRR7: forall[P3] 0.5*PC[P3,:Tal:WinterWeizen] >=
        PC[P3,:Tal:SommerWeizen] ;
'2.PXKART': PC[PE2,:Tal:Kartoffel] + PC[PE2,:Berg:Kartoffel]   +
        PC[PE2,PflanzKartoffeln] <=
            4.312;

{ pflanzliche Ertraege & Saatgut}
{ ---------------------------}
SET Ertraege/ErtragsVorgaben      {in 10'000 Tonnen}
        (Weizen'T01' (Winterweizen'00'/42.15 Sommerweizen'01'/6.03)
        Roggen'02'/2.01
        Triticale'25'/0.17 Gerste'T04' (Wintergerste'04'/21.36
        Sommergerste'05'/6.31)
        Hafer'06'/5.22 KoernerMais'07'/13.99 Kartoffeln'T09'/89.9
        (Kartoffel'09'  PflanzKartoffeln'29')
        Zuckerrueben'10' Futterrueben'11'/14.76 Raps'13'
        Bohnen'14'/0.1
        EiweissErbsen'26'/0.16 Gemuese'15' SiloMais'16'/153.001
        GruenFutter'T18'
        (Zwischenfrucht'17' Kunstwiesen'18' Naturwiesen'19')
        AlpWeiden'20'
        );
    Saat/ReproRate
        (Winterweizen'00'/0.2 Sommerweizen'01'/0.2 Roggen'02'/0.15
        Triticale'25'/0.17
        Wintergerste'04'/0.13 Sommergerste'05'/0.13 Hafer'06'/0.16
        Raps'13'/0.01
        );

COEF  Ertrag[Flaechen,P1] = maketable 'EPERTRAG' 1 ;
        bb(P5) = ( 0.01  0.0125  0.0125  0.0125  0.0125  0.0125)

VAR  YC(Perioden,Ertraege);            { Ertraege in 10'000 t }
        SC(P,Saat);                    { Saatgut in 10'000 t }
        SC09(Perioden);                { Saatkartoffeln }

MODEL
  'PY.C': forall[P1,&Ertraege] Ertrag[Tal,]*PC[,Tal] +
        Ertrag[Berg,]*PC[,Berg] = SC + YC ;
  { Ertraege zusammenfassen }
  PY: forall[P,#Ertraege] sum[*Ertraege] YC = YC ;
  { SaatGut }
  '--WDSC': forall[P1,Saat] SC[P1- 1,] = PC[,Berg]*ReproRate +
        PC[,Tal]*ReproRate;
  '65WDSC': forall[Saat] SC[PE5,] = PC[PE5,Berg]*ReproRate +
        PC[PE5,Tal]*ReproRate  ;
  { Spezielle Gleichungen fuer SaatKoernerMais und SaatKartoffeln }
  '--WDSC07': forall[P1] PC[P1- 1,SaatKoernerMais] =
            PC[,KoernerMais]*bb + PC[,SiloMais]*bb;
  '65WDSC07': PC[PE5,SaatKoernerMais] = PC[PE5,KoernerMais]*bb[PE5] +
```

73

```
              PC[PE5,SiloMais]*bb[PE5];
WDSC09:   forall[P1] SC09 = 2.7*PC[,PflanzKartoffeln] +
          2.7*PC[,:Tal:Kartoffel] + 2.7*PC[,:Berg:Kartoffel];

{ Direkte FutterMittel aus Ertraegen }
{ ------------------------------- }
SET Pfl_Futter/stfcCOEF
    (Futter1 (Weizen'01'/1 Roggen'02'/1 Triticale'25'/1 Gerste'05'/1
    Hafer'06'/1
    KoernerMais'07'/1 SiloMais'16'/1 Kartoffeln'09'/1
    FutterRueben'11'/1 Bohnen'14'/1
    EiweissErbsen'26'/1 GruenFutter'18' GruenFutter_total'19'
    Kleie'40'/1
    FutterGerstenMehl'41'/1 HaferAbfallMehl'42'/1 HaferSpetz'43'/1
    FutterHaferFlocken'44'/1
    MaisFutterMehl'45'/1 ZuckerRuebenLaub'46'
    ZuckerRuebenSchnitzel'48'/1 Melasse'49'/1
    FutterRuebenLaub'50' RapsKuchen'52'/1 Sommerstroh'53'
    Winterstroh'57' Abfall'60')
    Futter2 (ZuckerRueben'10' Z_siliert'47' F_siliert'51'
    Duerrfutter'54' TrockenGras'55'
    Silofutter'56') Futter_proteinreich'58' AminoSaeure'59'
    );
    BrotGet (Weizen'01' Roggen'02' Triticale'25')
    FuttGet/df (Gerste'05'/0.4 Hafer'06'/0.4)

COEF  Kart(P1) = (0.33  0.33  0.2  0.2  0.2)

VAR  FC(Perioden,Pfl_Futter);    { direkte & indirekte Futtermittel }

MODEL
    '--WMFC':   forall[P1,BrotGet]  0.025 * YC[P1- 1,]  >=  FC ;
    '--WMFC':   forall[P1,FuttGet]  df * YC[P1- 1,]  <=  FC ;
    '--WMFC09': forall[P1] Kart * YC[P1- 1,:Kartoffeln] <=
                FC[,:Kartoffeln];

{ Lager Sektor }
{ ----------- }
SET Z_Lager (Weizen'01' Roggen'02' Triticale'25' Gerste'05' Hafer'06'
            KoernerMais'07'
            Zucker'G10' Rapsoel'G13')
    Z_LagFuKons (SiloMais'16' DuerrFutter'54' SiloFutter'56')
    Pflichtlager/LagerKosten/LagerVorgaben/para
    (KriegsMehl'03'/46.62/41/0  SpeiseGerste'05'/51/0.4/0
    Haferflocken'06'/54.7/1.55/0
    MaisGriess'07'/56.7/3.2/0  Weizen'F01'/69.9/-/0
    Roggen'F02'/69.9/-/0
    Triticale'F25'/69.9/-/0 Gerste'F05'/69.9/-/0
    Hafer'F06'/69.9/-/0
    KoernerMais'F07'/69.9/-/0 Futter_proteinreich'F58'/69.9/-/0
    Zucker'G10'/90.8/28.5/0
    RapsOel'G13'/202.4/8.33/0   Reis'G30'/148.8/2.35/0
    KakaoBohnen'G31'/190.8/0/-
    KakaoButter'G32'/331.6/0/-
    )
    PfliLagSpez (AminoSaeure'59');

COEF  PfliLagPara[Pflichtlager] = (1 1 1 1 1 1 1 1 1 - 1 1 1 - -)
```

```
        PfliLagBnd[Pflichtlager] = (1 1 1 1 1 0 0 0 0 0 1 1 1 1 - -)

VAR  YS(P1,Z_Lager)   YZ(P1,Z_Lager)   YR(P,Z_Lager) { Zwischenlager }
     {Zwischenlager Rauhfutter }
     FA(P1,Z_LagFuKons) FS(P1,Z_LagFuKons) FZ(P1,Z_LagFuKons)
     FR(P,Z_LagFuKons) ;
     {Pflichtlager }
     YI(P2,PflichtLager) YJ(P2,PflichtLager)  YU(P2,PflichtLager)
     YO(P6,PflichtLager)  ;
     FU(P1,PfliLagSpez) ;

MODEL { Zwischenlager Sektor }
  HDFC:      forall[P1,Z_LagFuKons] FA + FZ = FS + FC ;
  '--SZFT': forall[P1,Z_LagFuKons] FS + 0.9*FR[P1- 1,] = FR + FZ ;
  '--SZYZ': forall[P1,Z_Lager]    YR[P1- 1,] + YS   =   YR + YZ ;
 { Importe und Pflichtlager Sektor } {255-259,262-265}
  '--SZYU': forall[P2,PflichtLager] YO[P1- 1,] + YJ  >=
              YO + YU + para;
 { Siloraumbegrenzung }
  '--SILKAP': forall[P1] FA[P1- 1,:SiloFutter]/0.65 +
              FR[P1- 1,:SiloFutter]/0.65
              + FA[,:SiloMais]/0.6 + FR[,:SiloMais]/0.6
              + FC[P1- 1,:Z_siliert]
              + FC[,:ZuckerRuebenSchnitzel]/0.9
              + FC[P1- 1,:F_siliert] <= 465;
 { Zielfunktion }
  '..ZMKOST': sum[P2,PflichtLager] LagerKosten*YU + sum[PflichtLager]
              LagerKosten*PfliLagPara*YO[PE4,] +
              sum[P2,PfliLagSpez] 90*FU = MIN;

{ Lebensmittel aus pflanzlichen Ertraegen }
{ ----------------------------------- }
SET Lebensmittel
     (KriegsMehl'03' Weizen'01' Roggen'02' Triticale'25'
      SpeiseGerste'05' Haferflocken'06'
      MaisGriess'07' Kartoffeln'09' Zucker'10' Rapsoel'13'
      Gemuese'15'
      Obst'21' Apfelsaft'22' Alkohol'23' Honig'24'
     );
     IndirektVerwend/e1/fcCOEF/e4/e5
      (Gerste'04'/2/1/-/0.95 (SpeiseGerste/2/-/-/-)
      Hafer'06'/1.92/1/-/0.95 (HaferFlocken/1.92/-
      /-/-) KoernerMais'07'/1.54/1/-/1 (MaisGriess/1.54/-/-/-)
      FutterRueben'11'/1/1/-/1
      (FutterRueben) Bohnen'14'/1/1/-/1 (Bohnen)
       EiweissErbsen'26'/1/1/-/1 (EiweissErbsen)
      SiloMais'16'/1/-/1.2/1 (SiloMais)
      )
     DirektVerwend/e2/e3
      (ZuckerRueben'10'(Zucker/7.15/- Zuckerrueben/1/-)
      Raps'13' (RapsOel/2.41/-)
      Gemuese'15'(Gemuese/1.27/-) GruenFutter'54'(GruenFutter/1/-
      DuerrFutter/-/7.8
      TrockenGras/6.5/- SiloFutter/-/2.4)
      );

COEF  cc(P1) = (33      29.7    26.4    26.4    26.4 )
{ZuckerRueben}
```

```
        dd(P5)  =  ( 1.28   1.15    1.15    1.15  1.15  1.15)   {Weizen}
        ee(P5)  =  ( 0.78   0.877   0.877   0.877   -     - )
        ff(P5)  =  ( 4.5    7.7     7.7     7.7   7.7   7.7)

VAR   GC(Perioden,Lebensmittel);           { pflanzl. Lebensmittel }

MODEL   { Ertraege + Zwischenlager >= Lebensmittel + direkte Futter }
        {WDYC01/WDYC02}
        '--WDYC': forall[P5,BrotGet] 0.975*YC[P5- 1,BrotGet] + dd*YZ -
              dd*YS >= FC + dd*GC ;
        WDYC03: forall[P5] GC[,:Weizen] + GC[,:Roggen] + GC[,:Triticale]
              + ee*YI[,:KriegsMehl] + ee*YU[,:KriegsMehl] =
              GC[,:KriegsMehl];
        '--WDYC': forall[P5,#IndirektVerwend] e5*YC[P5- 1,] + e1*YZ - e1*YS
                  >= fcCOEF*FC + e4*FA + sum[*IndirektVerwend] e1*GC ;
        '--WDYC09': forall[P5]  YC[P5- 1,:Kartoffeln] >= FC[,:Kartoffeln]
                  + 1.136*GC[,:Kartoffeln] + SC09;
        {WDYC10,WDYC13,WDYC15,WDFC54}
        WDYC: forall[P1,#DirektVerwend) YC >= sum[*DirektVerwend] (e2*GC +
              e2*FC + e3*FA) ;
        WDFC47: forall[P1] cc*PC[,ZuckerRueben] >= 1.8*FC[P1,:Z_siliert] +
              FC[P1,ZuckerRuebenLaub];
        WDFC50: forall[P1] 0.001*PC[,FutterRueben] >= 2*FC[P1,:F_siliert] +
              FC[P1,FutterRuebenLaub];

        { indirekte FutterMittel Aufspaltungen }
        'WDFC19': forall[P1] YC[,Alpweiden] + FC[,:GruenFutter] =
                  FC[,:GruenFutter_total];
        WDFC40: forall[P5] GC[,KriegsMehl] >= ff * FC[,Kleie];
        WDFC41: forall[P5] GC[,SpeiseGerste]+YI[,SpeiseGerste]+
              YU[,SpeiseGerste]
                  >= FC[,FutterGerstenMehl];
        WDFC42: forall[P5] GC[,HaferFlocken]+YI[,HaferFlocken]+
              YU[,HaferFlocken]
                  >= 4*FC[,HaferAbfallMehl];
        WDFC43: forall[P5] GC[,HaferFlocken]+YI[,HaferFlocken]+
              YU[,HaferFlocken]
                  >= 2.08*FC[,HaferSpetz];
        WDFC44: forall[P5] GC[,HaferFlocken]+YI[,HaferFlocken]+
              YU[,HaferFlocken]
                  >= 8.67*FC[,FutterHaferFlocken] ;
        WDFC45: forall[P5] GC[,MaisGriess]+YI[,MaisGriess]+YU[,MaisGriess]
                  >= 1.91*FC[,MaisFutterMehl] ;
        '--WDFC48': forall[P5] GC[P5- 1,Zucker] >=
                  0.49*FC[,ZuckerRuebenSchnitzel];
        '--WDFC49': forall[P5] GC[P5- 1,Zucker] >= 3.2*FC[,Melasse];
        '--WDFC52': forall[P1] 2.38*GC[P1- 1,RapsOel] >=
                  1.75*FC[,RapsKuchen];
        '65WDFC52': 2.38*GC[PE5,RapsOel] >= 1.9*FC[PE6,RapsKuchen];

{ Transformation: FutterMittel --> FutterWerte }
{ ----------------------------------------------- }
SET FutterWerte/yyh
        (Staerke'ST'/1 Hochw_Staerke'HS'/1 Protein'PR'/1
        Hochw_Protein'HP'/1 Sommerprotein'SP'/1
        KraftFutter'KF'/100 Hochw_KraftFutter'HK'/100 WinterFutter'WI'/1
        SommerFutter'SU'/1);
```

76

```
COEF  fw[Pfl_Futter,FutterWerte] = maketable 'EPFCWERT' 0;
      k09fw[FutterWerte] = (0 0 0 0 0 1 1 0 0)
      k09Per[P1] = (0.1 0.05 0 0 0)

VAR   FT(Perioden,FutterWerte);          { physiologische FutterWerte
      }

MODEL
   '--NTFT': forall[P1,FutterWerte] sum[Futter1] fw*FC +
      k09fw*k09Per*FC[,:Kartoffeln]
      + sum[Futter2] fw*FC[P1- 1,] + sum[Pflichtlager] (fw*YI +
      fw*YU)
      + sum[PfliLagSpez] fw*FU = FT ;

(*************************** TierSektor ***********************)
{ Tierbestand Gleichungen }
{ --------------------- }
SET Tiere/AminoSaeureAnteil
      (KuhBestand'60'
         (Red_SchlachtKuehe'61' (ReduktionsKuehe'72'
         SchlachtKuehe'73') LeistungsKuehe'62')
         Kaelber'64' (WurstKaelber'65' MastRind_1_Jahr'66'
         Aufzucht_1_Jahr'69' MastR_extensiv'74')
         MastRind_2_Jahr'67'
         Aufzucht_2_Jahr'70' Aufzucht_3_Jahr'71' neg_Selektion'68'
         junge_Kuh'63'
         MutterSchweine'80'/36.8 SchlachtSchweine'82'/8.8
         ReduktionsSchweine'81'/18.7
         MutterPoulets'84'/1.32 Poulets'86'/0.11
         ReduktionsPoulets'85'/0.22 MutterHennen'88'/1.56
         Hennen'90'/1.56 ReduktionsHennen'89'/0.26 Pferde'92'
         Schafe'93' Ziegen'94'
      );
   MutterTiere (MutterSchweine'82' MutterPoulets'86' MutterHennen'90')
   Aufzucht (MastRind_1_Jahr'66' (MastRind_2_Jahr) Aufzucht_1_Jahr'70'
         (Aufzucht_2_Jahr)
         Aufzucht_2_Jahr'71' (Aufzucht_3_Jahr));

COEF  gg[MutterTiere,P1] =
         (16.75 22.1 25 17 17, 33.6 33.6 33.6 33.6 33.6,
         42.9 42.9 42.9 42.9 42.9)
      hh[MutterTiere,P1] =
         (16.75 22.1 25 17 17, 144  144  144  144  144 ,
         65.6 65.6 65.6 65.6 65.6)
      xx[P1] = (1 0 0 0 0)

VAR   PL(Perioden,Tiere);               { TierBestaende in 100'000
Stk }

MODEL  { Rinder Sektor }{20-37}
   LZPL62: forall[P1] PL[,:KuhBestand] = PL[,:Red_SchlachtKuehe] +
         PL[,:LeistungsKuehe] ;
   LZPL61: forall[P1] PL[,:Red_SchlachtKuehe] =
         PL[,:ReduktionsKuehe] + PL[,:SchlachtKuehe] ;
   LZPL65: forall[P1] PL[,:Kaelber] >= PL[,:WurstKaelber] +
         PL[,:MastRind_1_Jahr]
         + PL[,:Aufzucht_1_Jahr] + PL[,:MastR_extensiv] ;
   '--LZPL': forall[P1,#Aufzucht] PL[P1- 1,] = sum[*Aufzucht] PL ;
```

77

```
LZPL68: forall[P1] 0.1837*PL[,Aufzucht_3_Jahr] =
        PL[,neg_Selektion];
LZPL63: forall[P1] 0.8163*PL[,Aufzucht_3_Jahr] = PL[,junge_Kuh];
LZPL64: forall[P1] 0.9*PL[,LeistungsKuehe] + 0.9*PL[,junge_Kuh] =
        PL[,:Kaelber];
{'--LZPL69': forall[P2] PL[P2- 1,Aufzucht_1_Jahr] =
        0.266*PL[P2+2,:KuhBestand];}
'02LZPL69': PL[PE0,Aufzucht_2_Jahr] <= 0.266*PL[PE2,:KuhBestand];
'03LZPL69': PL[PE0,Aufzucht_1_Jahr] = 0.266*PL[PE3,:KuhBestand];
'14LZPL69': PL[PE1,Aufzucht_1_Jahr] = 0.266*PL[PE4,:KuhBestand];
'25LZPL69': PL[PE2,Aufzucht_1_Jahr] = 0.266*PL[PE5,:KuhBestand];
'35LZPL69': PL[PE3,Aufzucht_1_Jahr] = 0.266*PL[PE5,:KuhBestand];
'45LZPL69': PL[PE4,Aufzucht_1_Jahr] = 0.266*PL[PE5,:KuhBestand];
'55LZPL69': PL[PE5,Aufzucht_1_Jahr] = 0.266*PL[PE5,:KuhBestand];
'--LZPL60': forall[P1] xx*PL[P1- 1,:KuhBestand] +
        (1-xx)*PL[P1- 1,:LeistungsKuehe]
        + PL[P1- 1,:junge_Kuh] = PL[,:KuhBestand] +
        xx*PL[P1- 1,:ReduktionsKuehe]
        + xx*PL[P1- 1,:SchlachtKuehe];
LZPL73: forall[P1] 0.2247*PL[,:KuhBestand] = PL[,SchlachtKuehe];
{ Weitere Tierbestandes-Gleichungen } {32-37}
LZPL: forall[P1,MutterTiere] hh*PL + gg*PL[,MutterTiere+2] =
        PL[,MutterTiere+1];
'--LZPX': forall[P1,MutterTiere] PL[P1- 1,] =
        PL + PL[,MutterTiere+2];

{ Angebot aus tierischen Produkten }
{ ----------------------------- }
SET Ti_Lebensmittel/L
    (Milch'T62'
        (VollMilch'62'/1 FutterMilch'F62'/1 Butter_direkt'72'/24
            (Butter'75' MagerMilch_Indu'80'/0.047 MagerMilch'77'/0.047
            MagerMilchFuetterung'F77'/0.047
            MagerMilch_Pulver'76'/0.517
            FutterMagerMilc'F76'/0.517)
        Kaese'78'/12.3 (Butter_Kaeserei'73'/8.0)
        Kaese_ein_Viertel_fett'79'/18.05
        (Butter_ein_Viertel_fett'74'/1.54)
        ) ButterMilch'F75' Schotte'F78' FleischKnochenMehl'F99'
    KalbsFleisch'65' RindsFleisch'67' SchweineFleisch'82'
    Gefluegel'86' Eier'90'
    PferdeFleisch'92' SchafsFleisch'93' ZiegenFleisch'94'
    Innereien'97' Tier_Fette'98'
    Fleisch_total'99' Wild'95' Fisch'96'
    );
TiLeMil/L1
    (Butter'74' (Butter_direkt/1 Butter_Kaeserei/1
                Butter_ein_Viertel_fett/1)
        ButterMilch'75' (Butter_direkt/1.75 Kaese/0.25
                Kaese_ein_Viertel_fett/1.2987)
        Schotte'78' (Kaese/11.24 Kaese_ein_Viertel_fett/14.49)
    );
TiLe_Aus/L2
    (Eier'90' (Hennen/0.132)
        Fleisch_total'99'
        (RindsFleisch'67'/1 (Red_SchlachtKuehe/2.06
            MastRind_2_Jahr/2.13 neg_Selektion/2.13
            MastR_extensiv/1.6) SchweineFleisch'82'/1
```

```
        (MutterSchweine/0.45 ReduktionsSchweine/0.96
        SchlachtSchweine/0.656) Gefluegel'86'/1 (MutterPoulets/0.013
        ReduktionsPoulets/0.012
        Poulets/0.0085 MutterHennen/0.01 Hennen/0.01
        ReduktionsHennen/0.01)
        PferdeFleisch'92'/1 (Pferde/0.195)  SchafsFleisch'93'
        (Schafe/0.175)
        ZiegenFleisch'94'/1 (Ziegen/0.09) Innereien'G97'/1
        (Red_SchlachtKuehe/0.3
        WurstKaelber/0.08 MastRind_2_Jahr/0.25 neg_Selektion/0.25
        MastR_extensiv/0.08
        MutterSchweine/0.026 ReduktionsSchweine/0.0552
        SchlachtSchweine/0.03
        Pferde/0.015 Schafe/0.019 Ziegen/0.006) Tier_Fette'G98'/1
        (Red_SchlachtKuehe/0.25
        WurstKaelber/0.005 MastRind_2_Jahr/0.15 neg_Selektion/0.15
        MastR_extensiv/0.033
        MutterSchweine/0.03 ReduktionsSchweine/0.06
        SchlachtSchweine/0.05 Pferde/0.015)
    )
  );
  TiLe_Out/L3/L4/L5
    (Milch'62' (LeistungsKuehe/37.55/35.55/33.55
     junge_Kuh/37.55/35.55/33.55
     Ziegen/3.1/3.1/3.1) KalbsFleisch'65'
     (WurstKaelber/0.51/0.33/0.33)
    );

    Ti_Futter (FutterMilch'F62' MagerMilchFuetterung'F77'
               FutterMagerMilc'F76'
               ButterMilch'F75' Schotte'F78'
               FleischKnochenMehl'F99');

COEF  jj[P1] = (0.38  0.38  0.35  0.35  0.35)
      ll[P1] = (0.3  0.23  0.21  0.19  0.19)
      mm[P1] = (0.0001  0.07  0.1  0.13  0.13)
      nn[P1] = (0.27  0.29  0.33  0.33  0.33)
VAR   GL(Perioden,Ti_Lebensmittel);

MODEL  { Milch Angebot } {283-287,310,316-321,323}
  WDGL: forall[P1,#Ti_LebensMittel] GL = sum[*Ti_LebensMittel] L*GL;
  WDFL: forall[P1,#TiLeMil] sum[*TiLeMil] L1*GL  =  GL ;
  WMGL72: forall[P1] GL[,VollMilch] >= 0.25*GL[,:Milch];
  WXGL72: forall[P1] GL[,VollMilch] <= nn*GL[,:Milch];
  WMGL75: forall[P1] 24*GL[,:Milch:Butter_direkt] >= jj*GL[,:Milch];
  WMGL78: forall[P1] 12.3*GL[,:Milch:Kaese] >= ll*GL[,:Milch];
  WMGL79: forall[P1] 18.05*GL[,:Milch:Kaese_ein_Viertel_fett] >=
          mm*GL[,:Milch];
  { Fleisch Angebot } {9-19} {Achtung: Gl.namen LYGL97/98 werden
    mittels File EP1.INC generiert}
  LYPL: forall[P1,#TiLe_Aus] sum[*TiLe_Aus] L2*PL  = GL ;
  '1.LYPL': forall[#TiLe_Out] sum[*TiLe_Out] L3*PL[PE1,] = GL[PE1,] ;
  '2.LYPL': forall[#TiLe_Out] sum[*TiLe_Out] L4*PL[PE2,] = GL[PE2,] ;
  LYPL: forall[P8,#TiLe_Out] sum[*TiLe_Out] L5*PL = GL ;

{ Futternachfrage der Tiere }
{ ----------------------- }
SET heikle_Tiere (SchlachtSchweine MutterPoulets Poulets MutterHennen
```

79

```
                        Hennen Pferde)
         SpezialFutter (Weizen'01' Gerste'05' Hafer'06' Koernermais'07'
                        Trockengras'55')

COEF
   Ti_FutterWert[Ti_Futter,Futterwerte] = maketable 'EPFLWERT' 0;
   Spez_Anteil[heikle_Tiere,SpezialFutter] = maketable 'EPFUSPEZ' 0;
   yy1[Tiere,FutterWerte] = maketable 'EPTIER1' 0;
   yy2[Tiere,FutterWerte] = maketable 'EPTIER2' 0;
   yy35[Tiere,FutterWerte] = maketable 'EPTIER35' 0;

   kk(FutterWerte,P1) = (1  1  1  1  1
                         1  1  1  1  1
                         1  1  1  1  1
                         0.9 0.8 0.8 0.7 0.7   {HP}
                         -  -  -  -  -
                         1  1  1  1  1
                         1 0.9 0.8 0.7 0.7     {HK}
                         1  1  1  1  1
                         1  1  1  1  1 )

VAR   DT(Perioden,Futterwerte);

MODEL
   NDFT: forall[P1,FutterWerte] FT + sum[Ti_Futter] Ti_FutterWert * GL
         >= kk*DT ;
   NDFTSP: forall[P1] 0.95*FT[,Sommerprotein] >= DT[,Sommerprotein] ;
   '1.LTDT': forall[FutterWerte] sum[#&Tiere] yy1 * PL[PE1,] =
             yyh*DT[PE1,] ;
   '2.LTDT': forall[FutterWerte] sum[#&Tiere] yy2 * PL[PE2,] =
             yyh*DT[PE2,] ;
   LTDT: forall[P8,FutterWerte] sum[#&Tiere] yy35 * PL = yyh*DT ;
   LTDT59: forall[P1]  sum[Tiere] AminoSaeureAnteil*PL >=
           FU[,AminoSaeure];
   NMFC: forall[P1,SpezialFutter] sum[heikle_Tiere] Spez_Anteil*PL <=
         FC + YI + YU ;
         {Operand der Gleichung 5.NMFC01 im File EP1.INC determiniert}

(************** Ernaehrungs & Rationen Sektor ****************)
SET Rationen/Lager/RationenBound/para1 =
     (Pfl_Rationen'CC'
       (KriegsMehl'C03'/-/9/1 SpeiseGerste'C05'/0.5/-/1
        Haferflocken'C06'/0.52/1.5/1
        MaisGriess'C07'/0.649/1.5/1 Kartoffeln'C09'/-/-/1
        ZuckerRation'C10'/-/-/1 Oel'C13'/-/-/1 Gemuese'C15'/-/1
        Obst'C21'/-/-/1
        Apfelsaft'C22'/-/-/1 Alkohol'C23'/-/-/1 Honig'C24'/-/-/1
        Reis'C30'/1/-/0
        KakaoBohnen'C31'/1/-/0  KakaoButter'C32'/1/-/0
        )
      Ti_Rationen'LL'
       (Vollmilch'L62' Magermilch'L77' Magermilch_Pulver'L76'
        Butter'L75' Kaese'L78'
        Kaese_ein_Viertel_fett'L79' KalbsFleisch'L65'
        RindsFleisch'L67' SchweineFleisch'L82'
        Eier'L90' Gefluegel'L86' PferdeFleisch'L92'
        SchafsFleisch'L93' ZiegenFleisch'L94'
        Wild'L95' Fisch'L96' Innereien'L97' Tier_Fette'L98'
```

80

```
              Fleisch_total'L99'
            )
         );
    Ti_RatSpez
           (Vollmilch'L62' Magermilch'L77' Magermilch_Pulver'L76'
           Butter'L75' Kaese'L78'
           Kaese_ein_Viertel_fett'L79' Eier'L90' Tier_Fette'L98'
           Fleisch_total'L99'
              (KalbsFleisch'L65' RindsFleisch'L67' SchweineFleisch'L82'
              Gefluegel'L86'
              PferdeFleisch'L92' SchafsFleisch'L93' ZiegenFleisch'L94'
              Wild'L95' Fisch'L96'
              Innereien'L97'));
    LRationen (Zucker'C10' (ZuckerRation) RapsOel'C13' (Oel));
    Physio_Bestimmungen/pb/pg
           (Mehl'C03'/-/0.05333(KriegsMehl/1000/-) Oel'C13'/-/0.03333
           (Oel/10000/- Tier_Fette/10000/-)
           Milch'C62'/-/0.1(VollMilch/1000/- MagerMilch/1000/-)
           Butter'L75'/-/0.03333(Butter/10000/-) Kaese'L78'/-/0.02
           (Kaese/10000/-
           Kaese_ein_Viertel_fett/10000/-) Eier'L90'/-/0.0466
           (Eier/10000/-) Fleisch'L99'/-
           /0.2(Fleisch_total/10000/-)
           );
    Naehrstoffe/Kal_Anteil/Kal_Part (Kalorien'TK' Proteine'TP'/4/0.1
           Fette'TF'/9/0.2
           Sichtb_Fette'TV' Kohlenhydrate'TC'/4/0.4)
COEF   { Naehrstoffgehalte je Lebensmittel }
       NaehrWertGehalt[Rationen,Naehrstoffe] = MakeTable 'EPNAWERT' 0;
       LagerSpez[Pfl_Rationen] = (1 1 1 1 1 1 1 1 1 1 1 1 - -)

VAR    R(Perioden,Rationen);{ Pflanzl. Lebensmittelrationen }
       NC(Perioden,Naehrstoffe);        { Pflanzl. Naehrstoffe }
       NL(Perioden,Naehrstoffe);        { Tierische Naehrstoffe }
       NT(Perioden,Naehrstoffe);        { Naehrstoffe total }

MODEL
    { Pflanzliche & tierische Lebensmittel Rationen } {138-152,153-171}
    RMG: forall[P1,Pfl_Rationen] GC + Lager*LagerSpez*YI + Lager*YU >=
         7.56*R ;
    '--RMG': forall[P1,#LRationen] GC[P1- 1,] + YI + YU + YZ >= YS +
         sum[*LRationen] 7.56*R;
    RMR: forall[P1,&Ti_RatSpez] GL >= 7.56 * R ;
    RMR: forall[P1,#Ti_RatSpez] sum[*Ti_RatSpez] GL = 7.56 * R ;
    { Pflanzliche & tierische Naehrstoffe } {91-95,96-100}
    NTNC: forall[P2,Naehrstoffe] sum[Pfl_Rationen]
             NaehrWertGehalt*R/1000 = NC/1000 ;
    '5.NTNC': forall[Naehrstoffe] sum[Pfl_Rationen]
             para1*NaehrWertGehalt*R[PE5,]/1000
             = NC[PE5,]/1000 ;
    NTNL: forall[P1,Naehrstoffe] sum[Ti_Rationen]
             NaehrWertGehalt*R/1000 = NL/1000 ;
    { Naehrstoffe total }
    'NT': forall[P1,Naehrstoffe] NC + NL = NT ;
{NTCARB/NTFETT/NTFETV/NTKALO/NTPROT}
    NMNLTP: forall[P1] NL[,Proteine] >= 0.3*NT[,Proteine];
    NMNT: forall[P1,NaehrStoffe] Kal_Anteil * NT >=
             Kal_Part*NT[,Kalorien];
```

```
NMNTOV: forall[P1] NT[,Sichtb_Fette]  >=  0.45*NT[,Fette];
NXRC09: forall[P2] 1000*R[,:Kartoffeln] + 0.65*NT[,Kalorien] <=
        68000;
'5.NXRC09': 1000*R[PE5,:Kartoffeln] + 0.6*NT[PE5,Kalorien] <=
        68000;
NXRC62: forall[P1] 1000*R[,Vollmilch] + 1000*R[,MagerMilch] +
        0.2*NT[,Kalorien] <= 39000;
   NMR: forall[P1,#Physio_Bestimmungen] sum[*Physio_Bestimmungen] pb*R
        >= pg*NT[,Kalorien];
{ Zweite Zielfunktion  }
'..ZXKALO': NC[PE5,Kalorien] + NL[PE5,Kalorien] = MAX;

(*************** Stabilisierungs Gleichungen ****************)
SET Tierel (MastRind_1_Jahr'66' MastRind_2_Jahr'67'
SchlachtSchweine'82' Poulets'86' Hennen'90'
           Pferde'92' Schafe'93' Ziegen'94')
        P9/brotgetreideRHS (PE2/12.5  PE4/14.8)
     stgc_Lebensmittel(Zucker'10' Rapsoel'13'  Obst'21'  Apfelsaft'22'
                 Alkohol'23' Honig'24')
     stgca_Lebensmittel(Roggen'02' SpeiseGerste'05' Haferflocken'06')
     stgcb_Lebensmittel(Weizen'01' Roggen'02' SpeiseGerste'05'
                 Haferflocken'06' MaisGriess'07'
                 Kartoffeln'09')
     styu_LebensMittel(Weizen'01' Roggen'02')
     Futter3 (Z_siliert'47' F_siliert'51' Sommerstroh'53'
              Duerrfutter'54'  TrockenGras'55'
              Silofutter'56')

COEF fc57[P1] = (5  15  15  15  15)
     styuCOEF(styu_LebensMittel,P2) = ( 0.78  0.87  0.87  0.87
                                        0.78  0.87  0.87  0.87)
MODEL
   { Futter }
   'ST.C03': forall[P9] PC[,:Tal:Brotgetreide] +
             PC[,:Berg:Brotgetreide] <= brotgetreideRHS;
   '56STFC': forall[#&Futter1] stfcCOEF*FC[PE5,] = stfcCOEF*FC[PE6,];
   '45STFC': forall[Futter3] FC[PE4,] = FC[PE5,];
   STFC57: forall[P1] FC[,SommerStroh] + FC[,WinterStroh] <= fc57;
   { Lebensmittel }
   '56STGC': forall[stgcb_Lebensmittel] GC[PE5,] = GC[PE6,];
   '45STGC': forall[stgc_Lebensmittel] GC[PE4,] = GC[PE5,];
   '12STGC': forall[stgca_Lebensmittel] GC[PE1,] >= 0.5*GC[PE2,];
   '45STGL76':  GL[PE4,MagerMilch_Pulver] = GL[PE5,MagerMilch_Pulver];
   '45STGL77':  GL[PE4,MagerMilch] = GL[PE5,MagerMilch];
   { ZwischenLager }
   '45STYZ': forall[Z_Lager] YZ[PE4,] + YS[PE5,] = YS[PE4,] +
             YZ[PE5,];
   STYU: forall[P2,styu_LebensMittel] GC + styuCOEF*YS >=
         styuCOEF*YZ;
   STYU05: forall[P2] GC[,:SpeiseGerste] + 0.5*YS[,:Gerste] >=
           0.5*YZ[,:Gerste];
   STYU06: forall[P2] GC[,:HaferFlocken] + 0.52*YS[,:Hafer] >=
           0.52*YZ[,:Hafer];
   STYU07: forall[P2] GC[,:MaisGriess] + 0.649*YS[,:KoernerMais] >=
           0.649*YZ[,:KoernerMais];
   { Flaechen }  {!!Achtung RelationsOperator}
   '45STPC': forall[#&Flaechen] PC[PE4,] = PC[PE5,];
```

```
'++STPMTL': forall[P2] PC[,:Berg:FruchtFolge] +
             PC[,:Berg:NaturWiesen] + PC[,:Tal:FruchtFolge]
             + PC[,:Tal:NaturWiesen] <= PC[P2+1,:Berg:FruchtFolge] +
             PC[P2+1,:Berg:NaturWiesen]
             + PC[P2+1,:Tal:FruchtFolge] +
             PC[P2+1,:Tal:NaturWiesen];
'56STSC09': SC09[PE5] = SC09[PE6];
{ TierBestaende }
'45STPL': forall[Tiere1] PL[PE4,] = PL[PE5,];

(******************** Bounds & Vorgaben ***********************)
COEF
    FlaechenMAX(Flaechen,P1) = maketable 'EPUPFLAE';
    FlaechenMIN(Flaechen,P1) = maketable 'EPLOFLAE';
    PflanzKartVorg(P3) = (0.35 0.5 0.5 0.5);
    TiereMAX(Tiere,P) = maketable 'EPUPTIER';
    TiereMIN(Tiere,P) = maketable 'EPLOTIER';
    EntnahmenMAX(PflichtLager,P1) = maketable 'EPUPLAGE';
    EntnahmenMIN(PflichtLager,P1) = maketable 'EPLOLAGE';
    fcKartoffeln(P4) = ( 30.01  38.2786   -  );
    fcZuckerR(P) = ( 0.0001 0.0111 0.0111 0.0111 0.0111 0.0111);
    fcZ_siliert(P1) = (14 15 16 16 16);
    fcTrockenGras(P) = (6  9.6   9.6  9.6  9.6  9.6);
    fcSiloUP(P) = (140  70   80   90   91   91)
    fcSiloLO(P) = (55   -    79  80    -    - );
    TiLebensMiMAX(Ti_LebensMittel,P1) = maketable 'EPUPTILE';
    TiLebensMiMIN(Ti_LebensMittel,P1) = maketable 'EPLOTILE';
    LebensMittelMAX(LebensMittel,P) = maketable 'EPUPLEBE';
    LebensMittelMIN(LebensMittel,P) = maketable 'EPLOLEBE';
    KartoffelnMAX(P1) = ( -  -  12  15  18);

MODEL
    BFLVO: forall[&Flaechen] PC[PE1,] = FlaechenVorgaben;
    BFLFX: forall[P3] PC[,PflanzKartoffeln] = PflanzKartVorg;
    BFLFX: forall[P3] PC[,GruenHafer] = 0.055;
    BFLUP: forall[P1,#&Flaechen] PC <= FlaechenMAX;
    BFLLO: forall[P1,#&Flaechen] PC >= FlaechenMIN;
    BYCVO: forall[#&Ertraege] YC[PE0,] <= ErtragsVorgaben;
    BYCLO: YC[PE0,FutterRueben] >= 14.5;
    BYCL:  YC[PE0,SiloMais] >= 130;
    BYIFX: forall[Perioden,PflichtLager] (para+1)*YI = 0;
    BYJFX: forall[P4,PflichtLager] (para+1)*YJ = 0;
    BYJFX: forall[PflichtLager] PfliLagBnd*YJ[PE4,] = 0;
    BYOUP: forall[PflichtLager] (para+1)*YO[PE0,] <= LagerVorgaben;
    BYUUP: forall[P1,PflichtLager] YU <= EntnahmenMAX;
    BYULO: forall[P1,PflichtLager] YU >= EntnahmenMIN;
    BYULO: forall[P4,PfliLagSpez] FU >= 0.001;
    BYUFX: FU[PE5,AminoSaeure] = 0;
    BYUFX: YU[PE3,RapsOel] = 0;
    BYUFX: YU[PE4,RapsOel] = 0;
    BYRF:  forall[Z_Lager] YR[PE0,] = 0;
    BFRFX: forall[Z_LagFuKons] FR[PE0,] = 0;
    BFZFX: forall[Z_LagFuKons] FZ[PE5,] = 0;
    BFZFX: FZ[PE4,DuerrFutter] = 0;
    BFZFX: FZ[PE4,SiloFutter] = 0;
    BFYZ:  forall[Z_Lager] YZ[PE5,] = 0;
    BPLUP: forall[P,#&Tiere] PL <= TiereMAX;
    BPLLO: forall[P,#&Tiere] PL >= TiereMIN;
```

```
BPLFX:  PL[PE0,:KuhBestand] = 8.68;
BPLFX:  PL[PE0,:ReduktionsKuehe] = 0;
BPLFX:  PL[PE0,:MutterSchweine] = 1.95176;
BPLFX:  PL[PE0,:MutterPoulets] = 1.22612;
BPLFX:  PL[PE0,:MutterHennen] = 0.46463;
BPLFX:  PL[PE1,:Ziegen] = 0.47;
BPLFX:  PL[PE5,:ReduktionsKuehe] = 0;
BFC:    forall[P4] FC[,:Kartoffeln] <= fcKartoffeln;
BFC:    forall[P] FC[,ZuckerRueben] <= fcZuckerR;
BFC:    FC[PE4,SiloMais] >= 30;
BFC:    FC[PE0,Z_siliert] = 35;
BFC:    forall[P1] FC[,Z_siliert] <= fcZ_siliert;
BFC:    forall[P] FC[,F_siliert] = 0;
BFC:    FC[PE0,DuerrFutter] >= 260;
BFC:    FC[PE0,DuerrFutter] <= 270;
BFC:    forall[P] FC[,TrockenGras] <= fcTrockenGras;
BFC:    forall[P] FC[,SiloFutter] >= fcSiloLO;
BFC:    forall[P] FC[,SiloFutter] <= fcSiloUP;
BFC:    forall[P1] FC[,Abfall] >= 10;
BGLUP:  forall[#&Ti_LebensMittel,P1] GL <= TiLebensMiMAX;
BGLLO:  forall[#&Ti_LebensMittel,P1] GL >= TiLebensMiMIN;
BGLFX:  forall[P3] GL[,:FutterMagerMilc] = 0;
BRCUP:  forall[P3,&Rationen]    R[,Rationen]   <= RationenBound;
BRCFX:  forall[&Rationen] (1-paral)*R[PE4,] = 0;
BRCUP:  forall[P1] R[,:Kartoffeln] <= KartoffelnMAX;
BGCUP:  forall[P,Lebensmittel] GC <= LebensMittelMAX;
BGCLO:  forall[P,Lebensmittel] GC >= LebensMittelMIN;
BNTLO:  forall[P2] NT[,Kalorien] >= 72000;
END
```

REFERENCES

Aigner D.J., "An Interpretative Input Routine for Linear Programming", Communications of the ACM, Vol. 10, Nr. 1, (Jan. 1967), pp. 23-26.

Anthonisse J.M., "Experiences with a Matrix Generator for Linear Programming", Haley K.B. (ed.), Operational Research '78, North-Holland Publishing Co., Amsterdam, 1979, pp. 950-954.

Ashton-Tate Ltd., "Learning and Using dBASE III plus", Torrance, Ca., 1985.

Bischop J. and Meeraus A., "On the Development of a General Algebraic Modeling System in a Strategic Planning Environment", Development Research Center, The World Bank, 1981.

Brandenberger M.B., "Implementierung eines primalen Algorithmus für das verallgemeinerte Transshipment-Problem", Dissertation, Universität Freiburg (Schweiz), 1984.

Burroughs Corporation, "Model Development Language and Report Writer (MODELER)", User's Manual No. 1094950, Detroit, Mich., 1980.

Control Data Corporation, "APEX-II Reference Manual", No. 59158100, Rev.C, Minneapolis, Minn., 1974.

Donaghey C., Dewan P. and Singh D., "A Beginner's Language for LP", Industrial Engineering Vol. 2.12, Dec. 1970, pp. 17-19.

Egli G. "Ein Multiperiodenmodell der linearen Optimierung für die schweizerische Ernährungsplanung in Krisenzeiten.", Dissertation, University of Fribourg (Suisse), 1980.

Egli G. and Kohlas J. ,(1981), "A Policy Model for Planning Alimentary Self-Sufficiency in Switzerland", BRANS, J.P. (ed.): Operational Research'81. Proc. 9th IFORS Int. Conf. on O.R., Amsterdam, New York, Oxford, 1981, pp. 311-322.

Ellison E.F.D., (1982) "UIMP: User Interface for Mathematical Programming.", ACM Transactions on Mathematical Software, Vol. 8, No. 3, Sept. 1982, pp.229-255.

Forrest J.J.H., "MAGIC/LAMPS: An Approach to Problem Solving", Working paper, CAP Scientific Ltd., London, no date.

Fourer R., (1983) "Modeling Languages Versus Matrix Generators for Linear Programming." ACM Transactions on Mathematical Software, Vol. 9, No. 2, June 1983, pp. 143-183.

Glover F., Klingman D., "On the Equivalence of some Generalized Network Problems to pure Network Problems", Mathematical Programming 4, North-Holland Publishing Co., 1973, pp. 269-278.

Glover F., "Creating Network Structure in LP's", Greenberg H.J., Maybee J.S., Computer-Assisted Analysis and Model Simplification, Academic Press, New York, 1981, pp. 361-368.

Greenberg H.J., "Graph-Theoretic Foundations of Computer-Assisted Analysis", Greenberg H.J. and Maybee J.S., (eds.), Computer Assisted Analysis and Model Simplification, Academic Press, New York, 1981, pp. 481-495.

Greenberg H.J., "A Tutorial on Computer-Assisted Analysis." in: Greenberg H.J., Murphy F.H., Shaw S.H.,(eds.) "Advanced Techniques in the Practice of Operations Research.", North-Holland, New York, 1982, pp. 212-249.

Haverly Systems Inc., "Omni Linear Programming System: User and Operating Manual", 1st ed., Deville, N.J., 1976.

Haverly Systems Inc., "MAGEN: Reference Manual", Denville, N.J., 1977.

Hürlimann T., "Reference Manual for the LPL Modeling Language.", Version 2, Working Paper, Institute for Automation and Operations Research, University of Fribourg, CH-1700 Fribourg, Switzerland, September 1986.

Hürlimann T., Kohlas J., "LPL: A Structured Language for Linear Programming Modeling, Working Paper, Institute for Automation and Operations Research, University of Fribourg, CH-1700 Fribourg, Switzerland, November 1986.

IBM World Trade Corporation "Matrix Generator and Report Writer (MGRW) Program Reference Manual", No. SH19-5014, New-York and Paris, 1972.

Jarvis J.J., Cullen F.H. and Papaconstadopoulos C., "EZLP: An Interactive Computer Program for Solving Linear Programming Problems", School of Industrial and Systems Engineering, Georgia Institute of Technology, Atlanta, 1978.

Katz S., Risman L.J., Rodeh M., (1980) "A System for Constructing Linear Programming Models.", IBM System Journal, Vol. 19, No. 4, 1980, pp. 505-520.

Ketron Inc., "MPS III DATAFORM: User Manual", Arlington, Va., 1975.

Knuth D.E., "The Art of Computer Programming.", Vol.1, 1973, p. 296.

Mills R.E., Fetter R.B. and Averill R.F., "A Computer Language for Mathematical Program Formulation", Decision Sciences 8, 1977, pp. 427-444.

M.I.T. Center for Computational Research in Economics and Management Science., "DATAMAT Reference Manual", 3rd ed., No. D0078, Cambridge, Mass., 1975.

Murphy F.H. and Stohr E.A., "An Intelligent System for Formulating Linear Programs", in: Decision Support Systems, Vol. 2, No. 1, March 1986, pp. 39-47.

Pasquier J., Hättenschwiler P., Hürlimann T., Sudan B., (1986) "A Convenient Technique for Constructing Your Own MPSX Generator Using dBASE II."

Angewandte Informatik Vol. 7, 1986, pp. 295-300.

Riggs J. L., Inoue M.S., "Introduction to Operations Research & Management Science.", McGRAW-HILL Kogakusha ltd., Tokyo, 1975, pp. 64-83.

Rothenberg R.I., "Linear Programming", North Holland, New York, 1979.

Rowe L.A., Davis M., Messinger E., Meyer C., Spirakis C. and Tuan A., "A Browser for Directed Graphs", Software-Practice and Experience, Vol. 17, No. 1, January 1987, pp. 61-76.

Schrage L., "Linear Programming Models with LINDO", The Scientific Press, Palo Alto, Calif., 1981.

SCICON Ltd., "SCICONIC/VM (Mathematical Programming System) and MGG/VM (Matrix Generator Generator)", OR Software Announcement in: OR-Spectrum, Vol. 6, 1984, pp. 125-130.

Sharda R., "Linear Programming on Microcomputers: A Survey", Interfaces, Vol 14:6, Nov.-Dec. 1984, pp. 27-38.

Sperry Univac Computer Systems, "GAMMA 3.4 Programmer Reference", No. UP-8199, Rev. 1,St. Paul, Minn., 1977.

Sunset Software, "LP83, A Professional Linear and Mixed Integer Programming System", Version 5.00, 1613 Chelsea Road, San Marino, Ca., 1985.

Steinberg D.I., "ALPS (Advanced Linear Programming System): An Easy Use Mathematical Programming Package", paper presented at ORSA/TIMS Joint National Meeting, Atlanta, Ga., 1977.

Index